Walking and Living in

YOUR
INHERITANCE

McDougal & Associates
Servants of Christ and Stewards of the
Mysteries of God

Walking and Living in YOUR INHERITANCE

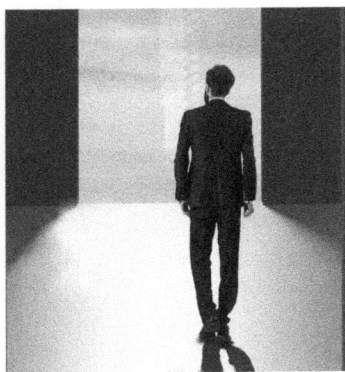

by

Dr. Abiola Idowu

Walking and Living in Your Inheritance
Copyright © 2022—Abiola Idowu
ALL RIGHTS RESERVED

Published by:

McDougal & Associates
18896 Greenwell Springs Road
Greenwell Springs, LA 70739
www,ThePublishedWord.com

McDougal & Associates is dedicated to spreading the Gospel of the Lord Jesus Christ to as many people as possible in the shortest time possible.

ISBN: 978-1-950398-71-3

Printed on demand in the U.S., the U.K., Australia, and the UAE For Worldwide Distribution

DEDICATION

This book is dedicated to all the saints of God, redeemed by the blood of Jesus Christ and sent to rule the Earth. Grace and peace be unto you from the Father of our Lord Jesus Christ.

Contents

Furthermore,
because we are united
with Christ,
WE HAVE
RECEIVED AN
INHERITANCE
FROM GOD,
for he chose us in
advance, and he makes
everything work out
according to his plan.
— Ephesians 1:11, NLT

INTRODUCTION

When we come to Christ, there is a complete disengagement from Adam and his failures. The curse, the punishment for sin, and the blood link to a fallen state all come to an end when we become new creatures in Christ. Many, however, fail to see that our redemption connects us directly to the inheritance of God. All that the Father has has now been put into our account. *"We have received an inheritance from God!"*

God's plans never fail. He stands His ground to see His purposes fulfilled. Therefore, nothing can hinder your inheritance. It is assured.

How do you get your inheritance? If you work for it, then it's not an inheritance. An inheritance comes to you because of your birth. God has made you a son or a daughter through Jesus, and whenever you see the estate of God, that is your territory. That belongs to you. It is your inheritance through Christ. What is God's estate? The Bible says:

> *The earth is the LORD's and the fullness thereof; the world, and they that dwell therein.* Psalm 24:1

Jesus also got His inheritance by birth. He said:

> *The father loveth the Son, and hath put all things into his hand.* John 3:35

> *All power is given unto me in heaven and in earth.* Matthew 28:18

And all that Jesus inherited is now ours. You are an heir with God and a joint heir with Christ (see Romans 8:17). But, if you don't even know what belongs to you, how can you claim it or enjoy it?

Our redemption will not be complete until everything that was lost in the Garden of

Eden is restored back to us. And that was a lot!

The conclusion of God about His creation was that everything He created was *"very good"* (Genesis 1:31). Sickness and disease are not good, so today marks the end of them in your life. Every breakthrough in life begins with an individual knowing the will of God. It is the will of God that establishes your rights and your proper inheritance in Him.

We can claim healing because healing and soundness of body, mind, and spirit is the will of God for you in Christ Jesus (see, for example, Isaiah 33:24 and Jeremiah 8:21-22). God said:

> *I will restore health unto thee, and I will heal thee of thy wound.*
> Jeremiah 30:17

Christ's victory over the devil does not just cover your sin; it also covers your health. It covers all *"the works of the devil"* (1 John 3:8). If Jesus reigns over all the Earth (see

Isaiah 9:6-7), there must be no sickness in His Kingdom. If you are part of the Body of Christ, then wholeness is your inheritance. The Body of Christ cannot be sick.

But you cannot get rid of sickness and disease in your body until you know the origin of it. Sickness and diseases gained entrance to this Earth through the sin of Adam and Eve. Until that moment, all was well.

It was never part of the plan of God for humanity to suffer. Then, however, when Adam and Eve came under the curse, they lost control over the Earth, and their archenemy, Satan, took over and punished them with all manner of afflictions.

Acts 10:38 shows us clearly that sickness is an oppression of the devil. Contrary to the belief of many people, in the story of Job, it was not God who was afflicting His servant (see Job 2:7). In fact, Job himself did not understand what was happening to him or why. He said, *"What? shall we receive good at the hand of God, and shall we not receive evil?"* (Job 2:10).

When Satan took over the affairs of this world, part of his program was to bring sickness and diseases (see Proverbs 29:2). In Satan's kingdom, people mourn. It was he who bound the lady of Luke 13:16 for eighteen years. This was the sad state of man when God decided to do a permanent repair of our destiny and sent Jesus to die for us (see Galatians 1:4).

The coming of the Lord Jesus was to buy back our bodies from the slave market of sickness and diseases (see Galatians 3:13). Jesus came, not just to save our souls, but also to save our bodies (see Ephesians 5:23).

As John 10:10 states, the devil came *"to steal, and to kill, and to destroy."* So, it is not the food you eat that makes you sick or what you inherited from your parents. It is the devil. He uses these other things to establish his claims, but they are not the cause (see Matthew 12:22 and Luke 11:14).

It was for this reason that Jesus rebuked the origin, the foundation of disease, so that men could gain liberty from the "afflicter," and that liberty is what Jesus purchased for you on Calvary.

As you read this book, get ready to take back your Eden. Read with an open mind, allowing the Spirit of the Lord to instruct you on the revelations He brings in these pages. If you do, I promise that your life will never be the same again.

Come with me now as we learn to walk in and live in the fullness of our God-given inheritance.

Shalom,
Dr. Abiola Idowu
Jacksonville, Florida

CHAPTER 1

CREATED FOR GOD'S PLEASURE

Thou art worthy, O Lord, to receive glory and honour and power: for thou hast created all things, and for thy pleasure they are and were created. Revelation 4:11

You and I were created for God's pleasure. This verse in Revelation shows that the purpose of redemption is to bring you to God's pleasure, His desires, His will, His determination. The main reason Jesus Christ came was to bring the pleasure of God to pass for all humanity.

Then said I, Lo, I come (in the volume of the book it is written of me,) to do thy will, O God.   Hebrews 10:7

Yet it pleased the LORD to bruise him; he hath put him to grief: when thou shalt make his soul an offering for sin, he shall see his seed, he shall prolong his days, and the pleasure of the LORD shall prosper in his hand.   Isaiah 53:10

We are created to fulfill God's desires, and His pleasure is to bring you pleasure. The challenge is this: if you don't know what His desires are, how can you claim them? When that is true, your reason for living will lose its meaning, and you will live like any other person.

What is God's pleasure? You cannot arrive at the answer to that question without going to the Master Plan that was used from the beginning to see how you came about.

God created the heaven and the earth.
Genesis 1:1

God didn't need the Earth, but He had a plan. According to the Bible, He created the Earth for it to be inhabited (see Isaiah

45:18). Inhabited by whom? Inhabited by man. Inhabited by you and me.

We know how that plan was truncated by the sin of Adam, but that did not affect God's purpose. He simply went back to His drawing board and put another plan in place. This one was eternal, everlasting. This time, instead of placing us in a physical garden, He placed us in His Son, Jesus Christ.

> *For in him we live, and move, and have our being; ... For we are also his offspring.* Acts 17:28

> *Therefore if any man be in Christ, he is a new creature: old things are passed away; behold, all things are become new.* 2 Corinthians 5:17

This plan of God is airtight. The enemy cannot enter and can only attack man when he comes out of this legal jurisdiction.

The pleasure of God starts with the new birth. If you have been born again, you have all the power in the Universe to become anything you wish in God (see John 1:12).

Enjoying the best of God is a function of believing right, not just living right. You will start living right when you start believing right.

When analyzing Revelation 4:11, the major concern is this: what is the pleasure of God? If we are created for His pleasure, His desire, His counsel, what does that mean? You can never understand this until you examine the Master Plan.

Nobody prayed for God to create the Universe. It was His desire to do it. It was part of His plan. Genesis 1:26-28 shows us the manifesto for Creation, but fulfilling it is based on man's faithfulness and obedience to the instructions God has given.

God said to the first humans concerning the tree of the knowledge of good and evil, *"In the day that thou eatest thereof, thou shalt surely die"* (Genesis 2:17). God trusted and believed in man, but man did not believe in himself, and in the end, he betrayed the trust of a loving God.

The ark of Noah was made as an instrument of rescue and salvation, but man's faithfulness was required to build it and then to enter into it, in order to be rescued. In the end, only eight people, of all those living on the face of the Earth at the time, made it into the ark and were saved.

The Law of Moses was given, and it required man's action and full obedience to it in order to be blessed. Unfortunately, because of the weakness of the flesh, man was unable to fulfill the requirements of the Law (see Deuteronomy 28:1-2 and James 2:10).

Eventually, God made a way out for man. This time, nothing was required of man except his willingness. Salvation was no longer based on man's ability, but on God's faithfulness and the obedience of Jesus on the cross (see Hebrews 8:7-12). This plan, that we call the New Covenant, was not based on the status of man, but on the status of Jesus. All that was now required of man was to exercise faith in the goodness and faithfulness of God, faith in what Jesus Christ did for us on Calvary.

God is faithful to save, to heal, to deliver, and to make righteous. In fact, it is because of His faithfulness that we are complete in Him. We have brought nothing to the table. Jesus did everything to bring the pleasure of God to pass in your life. With this, God had now achieved His desire for all mankind (see Acts 13:38-39).

All that God planned for humanity was poured into this new Man, making him the dream of Heaven on Earth. Your faults and failures do not affect God or His plans and purposes. They only affect you when you are not using your righteous stand with God. Until eternity, you are righteous, which gives you continual access to the Father. Without your input, He secured your healing, deliverance, and prosperity (see Isaiah 54:9-10, 14, and 17).

The promise now is:

> *I, even I, am he that blotteth out thy transgressions for mine own sake, and will not remember thy sins.*
>
> Isaiah 43:25

We are established in righteousness, and that brings us into victorious living. This victorious living is no more through human effort, but through Christ. You can get anything through Him by faith in what He has done for you (see 1 John 4:9-10 and 19).

Sin consciousness can rob you of your righteous stand with God and instill in you doubt and fear, an inferiority complex, and condemnation and guilt. This all comes when all the attention is on you and not on the price paid for you (see Hebrews 10:14). It is our thinking that determines our reigning. You cannot rise above your thinking, for *"as [a man] thinketh, ... so is he"*(Proverbs 23:7).

As Romans 5:13 shows, sin was in the world before the Law came, but it was not punished because there was no law. It was the Law that made sin a transgression. Before the Law of Moses came, Israel murmured against the Lord, and there was no punishment. They insulted God, and He showed them mercy. When there was no water, they contemplated going back to Egypt, and God still gave them water.

In those days, men lived for two hundred, three hundred, and even six hundred years because there was no consciousness of sin. There was no law to break, so there was no reason for punishment.

During this period, Satan was never an issue (see Romans 7:9 and 11). After the Law came and the people murmured, three thousand of them died that same day. The Law made sin a transgression (see Romans 4:15).

Thankfully, we are no longer under the Law, and that makes sin powerless (see Romans 6:14). If sin has lost its reign over you, then sickness and disease have also lost their grip.

Your purpose in life is not from you. It is from God, and He purposes everything according to His will. Through Christ, you now have access to God's throne. All the requirements for your enthronement have been paid, and all of God's assets are available to you. Therefore, it is no longer the devil who limits you; it is your own lack of faith in what Jesus has done for you, nothing more and nothing less.

Your purpose in life is the reason you are still living. God is waiting to see manifest what He has already put in you (see 2 Corinthians 4:7). It is there, waiting to bring forth fruit.

You are never empty, you are never poor, and you are never weak or sick. You are the righteousness of God, and you now have all that it takes to be great. The onus is not on you, but on Christ, who paid your price. Therefore, rise up now, and take advantage of your redemption!

Tell the devil, "I am no longer a sinner; I am a saint. Therefore, I cannot follow your directions any longer. You cannot control my mind, and you cannot put anything on my body. I am righteous now in Christ Jesus, and I know it" (see Romans 5:17).

All of this is the work of God's grace. It has nothing to do with your efforts. Your faith is the major ingredient that sets it into motion.

One of the important strategies of the enemy is to separate you from the love of God that we have obtained through Christ Jesus and make you feel that you need to do something to earn His love. Another of his tricks is to get your attention on something that doesn't seem to be working according to your plans, and he uses that to try to convince you that God doesn't care about you or your loved ones (see Mark 4:37-40).

Of course, it's all a lie. You are so valued that God has said *"even the very hairs of your head are all numbered"* (Luke 12:7). The Scriptures ask:

> *Who shall separate us from the love of Christ.*   Romans 8:35

The love of God is too deep to explain to the human mind. We are not accustomed to such deep insights (see Ephesians 3:19). It goes beyond our knowledge, and therefore, only the spirit can comprehend it. Your mind might think it is not real or even that it is absurd (see Romans 5:6-10).

The grace of the Lord Jesus Christ has removed sin and guilt completely from your account forever (see 2 Corinthians 5:19). Now you are blessed. Why? Because you are loved (see Romans 4:8).

The psalmist declared:

He hath not dealt with us after our sins; nor rewarded us according to our iniquities. For as the heaven is high above the earth, so great is his mercy toward them that fear him. As far as the east is from the west, so far hath he removed our transgressions from us.

Psalm 103:10-12

Jesus said:

I am the good shepherd: the good shepherd giveth his life for the sheep.

John 10:11

This is not normal. A good human shepherd loves his sheep, but it's because he is making money from raising them, or he loves to eat mutton. He would not want to give his life for them. But Jesus did, and we are the sheep of His pasture.

The moment you give your life to Jesus, He becomes everything you will ever need in this life. He completely takes your place in everything—including death, poverty, and disease.

God tested Abraham (see Genesis 22:12-13), and Abraham passed the test. It was Jesus who appeared that day on the mount of sacrifice. He came, not just as an angel, but to take the place of Isaac.

God knew that Isaac's blood was not pure enough to be a proper sacrifice. Now Galatians 4:28 says, *"We, ... as Isaac was, are the children of promise."* Jesus took your pain and sickness, your death and poverty, all because He loves you. He is your very life.

> *When Christ, who is our life, shall appear, then shall ye also appear with him in glory.* Colossians 3:4

Under the New Covenant, we enter into the dispensation of grace, passing from death to life, and we are now limitless and unstoppable. Why? See the answer for yourself in Colossians 1:13.

You are now under grace, and sin can never have dominion over you (see Romans 6:14). Therefore, Satan can never keep you bound. You will reign in life, for this is the provision of God that you access by faith in the finished work of Jesus Christ (see Romans 1:5).

It is through obedience to faith that God has forgiven me, healed me, and provided for all my needs. Remember, we are created for His pleasure, and God intended to bless us and make us His showpiece.

The Old Covenant was based on obedience to the Law and the sacrifices:

> *An altar of earth thou shalt make unto me, and shalt sacrifice thereon thy burnt offerings, and thy peace offerings, thy sheep, and thine oxen: in all places where I record my name I will come unto thee, and I will bless thee. And if thou wilt make me an altar of stone,*

thou shalt not build it of hewn stone: for if thou lift up thy tool upon it, thou hast polluted it.

Exodus 20:24-25

Under the New Covenant, it is faith in Jesus' finished work on Calvary that is required:

Knowing that a man is not justified by the works of the law, but by the faith of Jesus Christ, even we have believed in Jesus Christ, that we might be justified by the faith of Christ, and not by the works of the law: for by the works of the law shall no flesh be justified.

Galatians 2:16

Until you take hold of the principles of the Word of God, you cannot receive and enjoy your awesome inheritance (see Acts 20:32).

The challenge is this: a great majority of believers don't know that through redemption they have already arrived at their

Promised Land. What they are still fighting for has already been achieved. They just need to act on it.

The major fight we need to fight today is just to enter into the Lord's rest. This takes the renewing of the mind and staying connected to our Source by meditating on His Word and what it says about our current status.

Having faith in your works is never difficult. At least you know you've done them, and you feel you must be rewarded. The problem comes when all you do cannot satisfy God's standards. Even the best of us have flaws (see James 2:10). Therefore, you need help to get all that you desire, and that is where grace comes in:

> *Now to him that worketh is the reward not reckoned of grace, but of debt. But to him that worketh not, but believeth on him that justifieth the ungodly, his faith is counted for righteousness.*
>
> Romans 4:4-5

At one time or another, we have all questioned, "Why me? I'm not qualified for this, Lord." Then grace does its work.

The blessing of Abraham by Melchizedek was never based on Abraham's goodness. The high priest came to release over this man of faith a blessing from God. That is exactly where you now stand, under Jesus who was *"after the order of Melchisedec"* (see Hebrews 7:21-22).

All that God has done and is doing for us—sending His Son, healing us, and giving us His Holy Spirit—is because He loves us. Until you understand how much you are loved, you cannot enjoy what has been reserved for you (see Romans 8:32, Matthew 10:29-31 and 6:26).

Jesus died to give you everything. Through His death, He qualified you for all that your life deserves. Therefore, you must seek the pleasure of God now in the name of Jesus Christ.

You cannot be filled with the fullness of God until you know how much God loves you, and this is beyond religious talk. It takes a living and personal experience (fellowship).

Through Christ's love, God inputs unusual confidence into you and grows your faith. You then know that no matter what, God will show up for you, and He will never abandon you. Why? Because of Jesus (see Ephesians 3:14-20).

The prodigal son knew that no matter what he had done, he would still enjoy his father's love. Jesus has already committed me into the Father's hand, and there I am kept from every evil (see John 17:15). Meditate on His great love, and victory will be your testimony too.

You cannot afford to be a weakling, a failure, or a misfit. No, you are loved by God, and He is the ultimate, the Lover of your soul. You cannot earn God's love, but you can respond to it (see 2 Corinthians 5:14-15).

As children we learned to sing this little song:

Jesus loves me! This I know,
For the Bible tells me so;

Little ones to Him belong;
They are weak, but He is strong.

Refrain:

Yes, Jesus loves me!
Yes, Jesus loves me!
Yes, Jesus loves me!
The Bible tells me so.

As adults, we need to cling to this truth. Yes, Jesus loves me, and because of His love, I am an overcomer. He created me for His pleasure, and His plan was that I should prosper in life. You and I must now learn to walk in and live in the fullness of our God-given inheritance.

Shalom!

Righteous Decrees for Life

Father, in the name of Jesus Christ, whatever is planted in my life against Your Word is rooted out now in Jesus' mighty name!

Father, in the name of Jesus, I am destined to be the head and not the tail. By the authority of Your Word, I decree my promotion now in Jesus' name!

Satan, hear the Word of the Lord now. Take your hands off my health, my job, my spouse, my children, and my finances in the name of Jesus Christ. I am God's child, and He loves me!

CHAPTER 2

HEAVEN'S REJOICING

I say unto you, that likewise joy shall be in heaven over one sinner that repenteth, more than over ninety and nine just persons, which need no repentance. Luke 15:7

Heaven rejoices over a sinner coming to redemption. Why is that? The resurrection of Jesus was not a surprise to Heaven. It was all planned out as an act of *"the determinate counsel and foreknowledge of God"* (Acts 2:23). God knew it would happen, and therefore, it was not strange to Him.

Paul didn't consider even the raising of the dead to be *"an incredible thing"*:

> *Why should it be thought a thing in-*
> *credible with you, that God should raise*
> *the dead?*   Acts 26:8

Still, the thing that shakes the foundation of the Universe is the moment when a child of the devil is redeemed and becomes a child of God (see John 8:44 and 11:52). That is what causes Heaven to rejoice. Why? When a man or woman receives the same life that is in God, and His Kingdom and takes over his or her territory, that is reason for rejoicing. That changes everything.

When Jesus appeared to His disciple after His resurrection, He said to them:

> *All power is given unto me in heaven*
> *and in earth. Go ye therefore, and teach*
> *all nations, baptizing them in the name*
> *of the Father, and of the Son, and of the*
> *Holy Ghost: teaching them to observe*
> *all things whatsoever I have commanded*
> *you: and, lo, I am with you always, even*
> *unto the end of the world. Amen.*
>   Matthew 28:18-20

Jesus was the second Adam, and He was about to pass the power and authority He had received from the Father, through the baptism of the Holy Spirit, to those who loved and believed in Him (see Acts 1:8). This would forever change our status and make us invincible. All that Jesus had with the Father was to become ours.

Think of it! Jesus had all authority and all power, and because He said that He was the vine and we are the branches (see John 15:5), the authority that was in the vine would now flow to the branches. Jesus had become man, so that man could become like God. That is why Ephesians 2:6 is a reality today:

And hath raised us up together, and made us sit together in heavenly places in Christ Jesus.

We are the part of Jesus the world can see. We are the visible Christ, if you will:

Now ye are the body of Christ, and members in particular. 1 Corinthians 12:27

(Also see Ephesians 2:10.)

Let us think of it this way: we have been redeemed, but redeemed from what? Ours is redemption from the devil and his cohorts, redemption from poverty and failure, redemption from premature death, and much more. If there is a curse, your name is not on it (see Galatians 3:13-14 and Colossians 1:13). Why? Because the price was paid, the blood of Jesus was the payment, and His sacrifice in your stead was eternal.

You may remember that in Genesis 2:7, God breathed the breath of life into man. It was in that moment that man began to exercise dominion over all that was under him. It was then that he named the animals and called his wife Eve. In fact, it was then that his rib became active.

Sadly, man lost all of that when he fell because the life of God that produced all things in him had died. Now, however, God had a legal right to put the life back into man because man now belonged to Him through Christ (see John 3:17, 36 and 10:10 and 1 John 5:12-13). That new life removes you completely from the realm of death and the death-dealing power of Satan. But, just like software, you have to download the latest updates to enjoy all the benefits. That is done by your union with the Holy Spirit who indwells you.

Through redemption, all your limitations came to an end. They completely expired (see Romans 8:29-33). You have no need to beg for this blessing. It is yours. Take it!

In Philippians 4:13, Paul said:

I can do all things through Christ which strengtheneth me.

Yes, through Christ, you and I are legal masters of every situation, for we have a representative in the Godhead. He is the Head, and we are His Body. We have a representative in the Department of Justice in Heaven (see 1 John 2:1). We have a representative in the Health Department of Heaven, and a representative in the Finance Department of Heaven. And, through our

Representative, we are now more than conquerors. This spells the end of all pressure in life (see Hebrews 9:24).

The Scriptures go further and describe us as the very Bride of Christ:

> *For the husband is the head of the wife, even as Christ is the head of the church: and he is the saviour of the body.*
>
> Ephesians 5:23

> *For thy Maker is thine husband; the* LORD *of hosts is his name; and thy Redeemer the Holy One of Israel; The God of the whole Earth shall he be called.*
>
> Isaiah 54:5

If a man cannot provide for his family, he is considered to be *"worse than an infidel"*:

> *But if any provide not for his own, and specially for those of his own house, he hath denied the faith, and is worse than an infidel.* 1 Timothy 5:8

That is not to be our fate. We are born to be a pleasure to God, not misfits, not outcasts. You are God's masterpiece, a creation of excellence. You were packaged by Heaven, and deployed to the Earth as an agent of influence.

David sang:

> *What is man, that thou art mindful of him? and the son of man, that thou visitest him? For thou hast made him a little lower than the angels, and hast crowned him with glory and honour. Thou madest him to have dominion over the works of thy hands; thou hast put all things under his feet.* Psalm 8:4-6

David was not doubting. He knew what he was made of. That was why he could challenge the lion, the bear, and then Goliath. He knew that all things were under his feet.

The Creator did a perfect job on you too. He certified the originality of your person when He examined the work of His hands and, as we have seen, stamped it all *"very*

41

good" (Genesis 1:31). Nothing could undermine or demean what He had already exalted.

We all came here to planet Earth loaded and on a mission to make the Earth like Heaven. God put Himself inside of us, to make our job easier:

> *For it is God which worketh in you both to will and to do of his good pleasure.* Philippians 2:13

> *Now unto him that is able to do exceeding abundantly above all that we ask or think, according to the power that worketh in us.* Ephesians 3:20

Jesus said:

> *Ye are the salt of the earth: but if the salt have lost his savour, wherewith shall it be salted? it is thenceforth good for nothing, but to be cast out, and to be trodden under foot of men.*

*Ye are the light of the world. A city
that is set on an hill cannot be hid.*
                              Matthew 5:13-14

Remember, the Bible says that the counsel of God *"shall stand"* (Isaiah 46:10). You
are the counsel of God that must stand and
fulfill your God-given destiny.

There are principles of God that govern all
of creation, and understanding them causes
you to value yourself more highly. Let us
examine some of those principles:

1. **Every product of God's Creation has a
   mission in fulfilling His pleasure**:

   *And even things without life giving
   sound, whether pipe or harp, except
   they give a distinction in the sounds,
   how shall it be known what is piped or
   harped?*   1 Corinthians 14:7

   *For thus saith the LORD that created the
   heavens; God himself that formed the*

43

> *earth and made it; he hath established it,*
> *he created it not in vain, he formed it to*
> *be inhabited: I am the* LORD*; and there*
> *is none else.*   Isaiah 45:18

God set the sun in the sky to rule the day and the moon to rule the night. There are other things we see in the sky and don't yet know what they're there for, but He knows. He put them all there for a purpose. That's why your success and peace is included in your creation. Know this fact, acknowledge it, and declare it.

2. **The assignment for every part of Creation is determined by its raw materials.** The mission of each item of creation determines it contents and how they are packaged. Everything has been built to portray its assignment on Earth. Fish were not created like birds. The habitat and assignment of fish are very different from those of birds. God put

you on the Earth to reign and dominate the rest of creation (see Psalm 115:16).

3. God gave power to every aspect of Creation to manifest His glory.

The heavens declare the glory of God; and the firmament sheweth his handywork. Day unto day uttereth speech, and night unto night sheweth knowledge. Psalm 19:1-2

Even every one that is called by my name: for I have created him for my glory, I have formed him; yea, I have made him. Isaiah 43:7

There are also celestial bodies, and bodies terrestrial: but the glory of the celestial is one, and the glory of the terrestrial is another. There is one glory of the sun, and another glory of the moon, and another glory of the stars: for one star differeth from another star in glory. 1 Corinthians 15:40-41

You came here to manifest the glory of God, and your faith is paramount in that effort.

4. **There is no room for the malfunctioning of God's Creation, or the product would be functioning against its Source.**

> *I am the vine, ye are the branches: He that abideth in me, and I in him, the same bringeth forth much fruit: for without me ye can do nothing.*
>
> John 15:5

Plants remain fresh and productive if they do not rebel against the soil. It is the Source that was intended to sustain the product. The fish are forever kings as long as they remain in the water. Man is forever "undefeatable," as long as he is in Christ Jesus (see John 5:30).

5. **Every product of Creation has a language that sustains its existence.** The language of plants is water and

nutrients, the language of fish is water, and the language of man is faith. *"The just shall live by faith"* (Romans 1:17, Galatians 3:11 and Hebrews 10:38).

6. **The Word of the Creator is the strength and brains behind Creation.**

> *And God said, Let the waters bring forth abundantly the moving creature that hath life, and fowl that may fly above the earth in the open firmament of heaven. And God created ... every living creature that moveth, which the waters brought forth abundantly, after their kind, and every winged fowl after his kind: and God saw that it was good.*
>
> Genesis 1:20-21

This is the same thing He had said about the Earth; He saw it, and it was good. In Genesis 1:26, He spoke to Himself. Then came the creation of man (verse 27), and you are also *"very good"* (verse 31)

There is power resident in you, greatness you have not yet tapped. You are capable of doing what you have not yet done. God will give you opportunities, but it's your responsibility to depend on the Holy Spirit to act on those opportunities.

God knew what Adam was capable of doing, and He brought all the animals to him to name. When many see what God brings to them, they call it a "problem," but that's not right. Solve that problem with God's help. It is the problems you solve that announce you, not the ones you avoid.

Don't be a generational thief. Release what you carry. How can you do that?

1. **Maximize your time.** You become what you invest your time in. Don't spend your time; invest it. If I could see what you do daily, I could tell you where your investment is going.

2. **Set your goals.** If you aim at nothing, you will hit it. If you have set nothing as your vision, praying is useless. Setting

goals forces you to completely expose the true person you are. This will both help you find your limitations and discover your possibilities. Paul said he was ready (see 2 Timothy 4:6-8). If you don't understand what wastes your time, you will keep wasting it and never know the difference.

3. **Plan toward your goals.** Without planning, you are not living; you are just existing (see Proverbs 16:1 and 9). It's your responsibility to plan; God doesn't do the planning for you, but He will help you. Don't worry about the doing. Write down the plan (see Habakkuk 2:2), and then trust the Lord to help you bring it to pass. If you don't have a plan, you will fail. Many asked God to lead them, and God is asking, "Where?" That is why it's so easy for some to work several jobs. If you are not moving, direction is difficult. Planning will make you to know where God comes in. If you know you need Him to get there, you will never leave Him behind.

Yes, Heaven is rejoicing because of what Christ has done. You and I must now learn to walk in and live in the fullness of our God-given inheritance.

Shalom!

Righteous Decrees for Life

Father, in the name of Jesus Christ, I decree that every wonder packaged inside of me will begin to manifest in the name of Jesus. Let opportunities meet my abilities today and in the days to come, in Jesus' name!

Father, I receive wisdom for planning and execution in the name of Jesus Christ. I must not labor in vain again in Jesus' name!

Father, I decree that my heavens are open now according to Your Word in Jesus' mighty name!

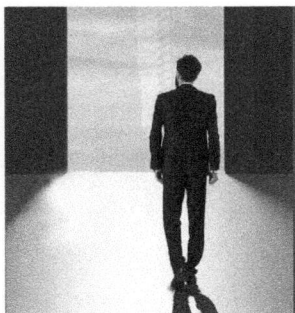

CHAPTER 3

THE AUTHORITY OF KINGDOM PLACEMENT

But without faith it is impossible to please him: for he that cometh to God must believe that he is, and that he is a rewarder of them that diligently seek him. Hebrews 11:6

Everything in the Kingdom is received and acquired on the platform of faith and not emotion. It is not only a matter of knowing what the Word says; it is also believing what the Word says and releasing your faith into it. When you know who God is, that He created all things and has the final say over everything here on Earth, that there is nothing impossible for Him to do, and that He communicates with us through His Word, then your faith is released into every word that comes from Him.

Understand that every word of God is covenanted. As far as God is concerned, what He says is an established fact, and nothing can change it. It is settled in Heaven, and your agreement settles it in the Earth realm.

Mary's reaction to the angelic announcement was: *"Be it unto me according to thy word"* (Luke 1:38). That put every biological process into motion, and Mary conceived by the Holy Spirit. Thank God the same Word that created Heaven and Earth is available to create your destiny (see 1 John 5:4-5). You have been divinely placed by redemption, and Ephesians 2:6 says you are *"seated together in heavenly places in Christ Jesus."*

You are sharing rulership with the Almighty. That is the highest honor in the Universe. You did not put yourself there, and there is no price that you could have paid to be placed there. Only grace could do that.

The Mighty One who ruled in the beginning, when everything was without form and void—the Holy Spirit, resides in you. Yes, you are a biological miracle.

However, every Kingdom blessing operates according to Kingdom principles. Many believers have been frustrated and disappointed about their faith because they thought they were standing on the Word and confessing the Word, but the results they expected were not there. "What's wrong with me?" I am asked many times. The answer is: there's nothing wrong with you. You just need to learn how the Kingdom operates so that you can enjoy its benefits.

Jesus Christ said, *"Unto you it is given to know the mystery of the kingdom of God"* (Mark 4:11). The secrets of the Kingdom are for its faithful citizens. The world will not have a clue. These secrets are reserved for our benefit. Everyone wants to enjoy the fullness of the blessing of God, but ignorance of what it takes can rob us (see James 2:5).

Matthew 28:18-20 contains the last words Jesus spoke to His disciples before returning to Heaven. There was no reason for fear and doubt, He said, for He was going to release His power upon His faithful disciples. He said, " *All power is given unto me in heaven and in earth,*" and since He was going to be with them, with all that power, they would experience that power as they went about evangelizing in His name.

If we stand together in prayer and fasting and issue decrees in the name of Jesus, but we never go out to tell others the Good News of Jesus and His sacrifice, then the mighty manifestation of God's power may not be there for us. But Jesus said, *"Lo, I am with you always,"* and the mystery of divine presence brought an amazing confidence to His early followers.

MYSTERIES OF THE DIVINE PRESENCE

1. **God's presence melts every obstacle, and you become untouchable (see Psalm 114:1-2 and 6-7).** Uzzah died for touching the sacred Ark. It was not the wood in question, but the Person it represented.

Now you have become the Ark. As you go your way, be conscious of this and the fact that you are not alone. The entire army of Heaven stands to back you up.

This was what Saul encountered as he was persecuting the early disciples. You dare not do that. Jesus stood up from His throne and blinded Saul. Realizing that some power that could not be challenged had gone into action, he asked, *"Who art thou, Lord"* (Acts 9:5). Jesus answered him, *"I am Jesus, whom thou persecutest"* (same verse). It was no longer an issue of persecuting Peter, James, or John. This was the Son of God who was now involved. Every child of God is loved by God, but very few are walking in His covenant through evangelism, which is the heartbeat of God.

2. **God's presence brings fullness of joy and pleasure (see Psalm 16:11).** And that is what you will begin to experience. Jesus said, *"When I sent you without purse, and scrip, and shoes, lacked ye any thing?"* (Luke 22:35). The disciples answered, *"Nothing"*

(same verse). When you go out in faith to evangelize, you escape every lack, for God Himself is committed to footing your bill. Why? Because He said, *"The labourer is worthy of his hire"* (Luke 10:7).

3. **God's presence establishes your peace and serenity.** Habakkuk 2:20 says, *"The LORD is in His holy temple; ... keep silence before him."* Every evil, every sickness, and every mountain must remain silent before Him, and His presence is with you when you go out in His name. This is not just when you want to go or plan to go, but when your commitment to go is already released with prayers.

4. **God's presence brings you glory and honor (see 1 Chronicles 16:27).** You cannot carry God's presence and not manifest His glory and honor. When Jesus was going into Jerusalem, people came out and spread their clothes and palm branches on the street for Him to walk over, and they shouted, *"Hosanna to the*

son of David: Blessed is he that cometh in the name of the Lord; Hosanna in the highest" (Matthew 21:9). But who was walking on those clothes? It was the donkey Jesus rode on. If He rides, you, too, receive the honor.

Jesus' name took Peter to places he was not known, and now it's your turn. You must be lifted up now in Jesus' name.

5. **God's presence brings you rest (see Exodus 33:14).** Biblical rest is not sleeping. It is completion. It is fulfillment. It is accomplishment. The Word of God says, *"My presence shall go with thee, and I will give thee rest"* (Exodus 33:14). The angry sea saw His presence and fled. The swollen Jordan saw His presence and was driven back. I am blessed to know His presence and carry it. I did not call myself to this work. God called me, He anointed me, and He sent me to help His people.

It was not because I had done anything extraordinary. It was all by His grace. His power is always with me to make a difference in my daily life. And God will do the same for you.

Imagine it. God called Moses, and the rod he had in his hand began to work wonders. That was not due to Moses' power. That was God at work. His power cannot remain on you and your destiny remain the same. You will be lifted up.

The Old Testament prophet Samuel told Saul, *"And the Spirit of the LORD will come upon thee, and thou shalt ... be turned into another man"* (1 Samuel 10:6). The only things that were physical that day were the oil and Saul. What went into Saul's life was beyond oil. And when that same anointing oil was poured on David, the same heavenly force came into him:

> *I have found David my servant; with my holy oil have I anointed him: with whom my hand shall be established: mine arm also shall strengthen him. The enemy shall not exact upon him; nor the son of wickedness afflict him. And I will beat down his foes before his face, and plague*

*them that hate him. But my faithfulness
and my mercy shall be with him: and in
my name shall his horn be exalted. I will
set his hand also in the sea, and his right
hand in the rivers.* Psalm 89:20-25

Something will be coming into you now
as you go forth to win others to Christ.
You will experience strong and unusual
manifestations of God's presence. Why?
Because you are on a mission for the
Almighty. Cry out to the Lord even
now, "Envelope me in Your power today, O Lord! Stir my heart for fruitful
soul-winning in the days ahead in Jesus'
name! Lead me to people whose hearts
are ready to be harvested in the name of
Jesus Christ."

CREATING AN ATMOSPHERE
FOR HIS PRESENCE

God is King, and He rules by decree.
When He decrees a thing, He then backs
it up with His power. This is a decree of

the watchers, that all men may know that God rules in the affairs of men (see Daniel 4:17). His decree over your life is that you shall be the head and not the tail, you shall be above only and not beneath (see Deuteronomy 28:13). This means that you are divinely placed. But in order to manifest your placement, you must first provide an atmosphere where God can manifest His promises (see Matthew 6:33).

The woman of Shunem provided the right atmosphere so that all of God's intentions could come to pass in her life. She said, *"I perceive that this man is a holy man of God"* (2 Kings 4:9). In this way, the atmosphere was provided for the placement to work. This woman had no personal agenda. She was just returning God's love.

You will enjoy the fullness of God's favor when you love what He loves. John 3:16 says, *"For God so loved the world."* God does not just love the Church; He loves the world. He loves the world because He loves Himself, and He wants to see Himself healthy and prosperous, winning at all times.

Nobody has ever seen God before, but we are created in His image and likeness. His commitment to man is the proof of His love for Himself. That is why you cannot fail, because God loves Himself. He loves Himself and wants to see Himself doing well. Therefore, He pours Himself out to man (see Genesis 2:7).

When man "messed up" and was separated from God, God decided to bring man back to Himself—all because of His love. If you love God and want to honor Him, bringing men and women back to God will be your top priority. He wants us all to share His rulership and dominion.

When man missed God's eternal purpose and left the place of honor and dignity, God could no longer see Himself, and He couldn't stand that. Since His eyes cannot behold sin, He sent His Son here to Earth to bring man back to God. Our redemption was made available through Jesus' blood that washes man as if his sin had never happened (see 2 Corinthians 5:18-20).

The Bible says, *"God was in Christ, reconciling the world unto himself"* (verse 19). The word *conciliation* means "to make one, to gain." So man was once one with God, gained by God, until sin separated him. Now the assignment of Jesus is to bring us together again as one with God.

"Not imputing their trespasses [sin] unto them" (verse 19). God did not just forgive us our sins through Christ; He wiped our sins out completely, as if they had never happened. There is nothing you can do or will ever do that Jesus has not already paid for.

The Bible says in Isaiah 53:6, *"The Lord hath laid on him the iniquity of us all."* Romans 4:25 declares, *"Who was delivered for our offences and raised for our justification [righteousness]."* As far as God is concerned, if you are in Christ, you are His favorite. Your record is clean with Him. There is no condemnation at all (see Romans 8:1). God looks at you and is happy with what He sees. If you realize this, you will keep yourself pure:

We know that whosoever is born of God sinneth not; but he that is begotten of God keepeth himself, and that wicked one toucheth him not. 1 John 5:18

God has given us the same assignment as Jesus had. Just as God was in Christ, He is now in you, reconciling the world to Himself. Therefore, you carry the anointing, the grace, the power, and the strength of the Almighty to bring people back to His image.

Our mission on Earth will remain incomplete until God's desire for humanity is achieved. He lost His children in the Garden of Eden, He wants them back home through the redemption provided by Jesus, and He is ready to share His fortune with anyone who will join Him on this mission.

The Bible declares that God wants all men to be saved. When you are on this mission, you command Heaven's attention, and your toiling ends (see Luke 5:5). There are fish in the ocean that will not come to your boat until you allow Jesus to use that boat. Then the toiling ends.

Yes, it is true that going out to make disciples of all nations involves money. Going is not cheap, but when you are committed to it, your heavenly Father pays the bills. He supplies everything you need.

Reaching out to the lost is not optional, and it's not the job of just a few. It is an assignment for us all that is proof that you love God.

Paul the apostle said that a soul-winner has an insurance policy on his or her life that no amount of money could ever buy (see 2 Timothy 4:3-5). When you recognize your call and commit yourself to it, this will be your portion.

Jesus said to His disciples, "If you go into any city or any house, and they do not accept you, *shake off the dust of your feet* as a witness against them" (Matthew 10:14). In so doing, you have literally placed judgment on that house or city. Even the dust of your feet is important.

So, stop complaining, and start winning souls by applying Kingdom principles. You are the envy of every nation, so don't languish in a corner somewhere. Announce God to this world, and see your destiny announced.

Ask God to help you:

- Lord, lead me in the days ahead to the lost. Help me not to keep my mouth shut, in the name of Jesus Christ. Show me how to serve You better in the name of Jesus.

- By the power of the Holy Spirit, I receive genuine passion for the lost now in Jesus' name.

- Father, I connect to the grace of favor, health, and honor for the sake of winning the lost in the name of Jesus Christ.

You cannot enjoy the fullness of God's blessing until you know that God's Word is equal to God's power and presence. It has no expiration date. It is as new and valid today as the day it was spoken.

The Bible says, *"In the beginning was the Word, and the Word was with God, and the Word was God"* (John 1:1). God is that Word, and with that Word He created all things. There is nothing that exists without the Word (see John 1:3). Even angels came into being by the Word. Creation by the Word was not just of this planet; it was of everything that exists.

The dominating force of the Word creates a turning point for everyone who believes it. The Word is so powerful that it controls the entire Universe (see, for example, Genesis 32:9-10, NLT). Your status has now changed. If God is the One who changed the life of Jacob by His mercy, take your promotion, healing, joy, and job now in Jesus' name.

From the time God spoke about the birth of Jesus, the Word went into action, looking for fulfilment by agreement. The Word persevered through the prophets, who stood against persecution, until eventually a young lady named Mary came into agreement with that Word.

From the time of her conceiving to the time Herod called for a census, to the time of the slaughter of all the children (when he was looking for Jesus), the Word prevailed over everything and everyone. The Word dominated every situation.

The wisemen could not explain why they were looking for a star. Astronomy could not get in the way. No science could get in the way. No government could get in the way. No people could get in the way. No emotion could stop the Word because of its dominating power.

> *He sent his word, and healed them, and delivered them from their destructions.*
> Psalm 107:20

> *So the word of the Lord grew mightily and prevailed.* Acts 19:20, NKJV

It prevailed over what? It prevailed over sickness, over failure, over stagnation, over satanic interruptions of every kind. Through God's Word, you can win today. You are out of every predicament now, no matter what or why in Jesus' name.

The Word of God is your turning point tool. Isaiah 43:18 declares:

Remember ye not the former things, neither consider the things of old.

Forget them. No longer consider them. Can that be right? Oh, yes! Definitely!

Only you can express what you are going through, for my experience is different from yours. There is no way I can express it like you, but it is important not to keep considering your past. The past is past, and there is a new way here now! There is a turning point. No matter what your past was like, you are free of it now in the name of Jesus Christ. Why? Because God promised, *"I will never leave thee, nor forsake thee"* (Hebrews 13:5).

I want you to see your life from a spiritual point of view, the way God sees it. That is the only way you won't consider the former things. We are born again to be a spirit and operate in the spirit realm. The physical realm is a slave to the spirit realm. It cannot stand as long as you do not agree with it.

You are a representative of the Spirit now (see John 3:7-8).

The spirit realm is eternal and does not have any limitations. The physical realm is temporal, and time controls it (see 2 Corinthians 4:18). The spirit realm is eternal, and the tool it uses is the Word of God (see John 6:63). The Controlling Force that created all things says, *"I will do a new thing; now ..."* That *now* is eternal. It has no time constraint.

The promise continued, *"I will even make a way in the wilderness, and rivers in the desert"* (Isaiah 43:19). Get ready for the unusual. There is a turning coming to you today in Jesus' name.

Life is controlled by the power of cause and effect. Without a cause, there is no effect. Many times, the cause is not physical. The effect, however, can be seen and felt.

For example, sickness and diseases are felt physically, but their causes are hidden. You cannot see ebola or cancer. You just see their effects. Without treating the cause, you are wasting your time dealing with the effects.

71

The boils on Job were not his problem. Satan had smitten him. Poverty is not the problem; it's just the effect of you being robbed (see Galatians 3:13). Stagnation is not the problem; it's the devil who came to steal, kill, and destroy (see John 10:10).

So, what is the cure for it all? After Jesus came, the Word says the works of the enemy are now destroyed (see 1 John 3:8). The Word also says, in 2 Chronicles 16:9, that God is committed to seeing you saved. His eyes are running to and fro throughout the whole Earth on behalf of everyone who desires to rely on and trust in Him (see 2 Chronicles 16:9). The phrase used here, *"whose heart is perfect,"* may be misunderstood if you don't read the whole story. When you rely on Him, your heart is perfect.

It is the nature of an apple seed to produce an apple tree and apples. The Word of God is also a seed (see Luke 8:11), and it is the nature of the Word to produce after its kind. Healing scriptures will produce healing fruits. Prosperity scriptures will produce prosperity fruits. Turning-point scriptures, when planted in faith, will effortlessly produce a turning-point destiny.

God said, *"Behold, I will do a new thing,"* but you did not ask Him for it. It's time to ask now and get your destiny back.

YOU CAN LIVE IN SOUND HEALTH

Redemption without sound health is a fallacy. It's incomplete. Before man fell, he was not sick, he was not poor, and he was not oppressed. As noted, the Bible tells us that all was *"very good"* (Genesis 1:31). Verse 26 says that Adam and Eve were created to dominate. If redemption is the restoration of all things, it must take us back to the state we lost. Nothing below that standard will do.

No wonder the Scriptures say, *"He brought them forth also with silver and gold: and there was not one feeble person among their tribes"* (Psalm 105:37)! When the children of Israel were delivered from Egypt, they came out with sound health and a wealth transfer.

73

Whatever you have lost is restored back to you now in the name of Jesus Christ.

Redemption is all about restoration. God said, *"I will restore health unto thee, and I will heal thee of thy wounds"* (Jeremiah 30:17). God's love is demonstrated in our soundness (see 1 John 4:8-10).

If you know what sin did to man, you will appreciate the price Jesus paid to redeem all men from sickness and disease. The good news is this: There is a solution to sickness and disease. Sickness need not be a death sentence. The pathway to freedom from sickness and disease is to be found in God's Word (see Proverbs 4:20-22). Let's look at this issue of sickness more thoroughly.

1. **Where does sickness come from?** The Fall of man licensed the devil to gain access to humans and exercise lordship over them. The Lord had said, *"The day that thou eatest thereof thou shalt surely die"* (Genesis 2:17). This meant that man would be separated from God and have another lord over his

spirit. He would live in darkness, disconnected from divine rulership (see Genesis 3:14 and 17-19). Consequently, man became Satan's food, for Satan became the god of this world and ruled tyrannically. John 10:10 says that Satan came to steal, kill, and destroy. After he came and destroyed the joy and peace of Job, he tried to blame it on God, as if God had ever done such a thing—killing Job's children and smiting Job himself with sickness (see Job 2:7).

A messenger said to Job, *"The fire of God is fallen from heaven,"* (Job 1:16). The devastation was also blamed on the Sabeans and the Chaldeans. But it was the devil himself who was to blame, as Acts 10:38 clearly shows us:

How God anointed Jesus of Nazareth with the Holy Ghost and with power: who went about doing good, and healing all that were oppressed of the devil; for God was with him.

(See also Luke 13:11 and 16.)

2. **What is the cure for sickness and disease?** For every problem, there is a solution. When man fell, God made a way of escape for him—if only he would not despise it and listen to God and not to the enemy. In Genesis 3:15, God said, *"It shall bruise thy head, and thou shall bruise his heel."* The common word here is *bruise*. It meant that the seed of the woman (Christ) would temporarily be punished, crushed, and struck on the heel, but the seed of the serpent would be crushed and struck on the head, which made it a permanent injury. The escape God provided was the bruising of the seed of the woman.

Isaiah 53:5 shows that we no longer have to suffer from sickness and diseases, for the price has been paid. The stripes of Jesus paid for everything. He has been bruised, and His death was a paralyzing force against evil (see Hebrews 2:14 and Matthew 8:17). Looking up is the answer to cancer, not more cancer research.

And as Moses lifted up the serpent in the wilderness, even so must the Son of man be lifted up: that whosoever believeth in him should not perish, but have eternal life.   John 3:14-15

Every poison of sickness, I command you, "Come out now in Jesus' name. I hold on to the price paid for our healing, the stripes of Jesus, and I receive my wholeness now in Jesus' name."

3. **How do I apply the provision?** Everything God promised you can only be ratified by faith with your confession. The Bible says:

The tongue of the wise is health.
                    Proverbs 12:18

Life and death are in the power of the tongue.   Proverbs 18:21

For he that will love life, and see good days, let him refrain his tongue

77

from evil, and his lips that they speak no guile. 1 Peter 3:10

You cannot afford to be speaking sickness if what you need is health. This is not a joke. The Bible says, *"Let the weak say, I am strong"* (Joel 3:10). Read the healing scriptures, meditate on them, and then speak them forth.

Jesus said, *"I give you a mouth and wisdom, which all your adversaries shall not be able to gainsay nor resist"* (Luke 21:15). Amen!

4. **What do I do after the application?** The Bible says, *"After ye have done the will of God, ye might receive the promise"* (Hebrews 10:36). So, what is the will of God? It is His Word (see 1 Thessalonians 5:18). In Matthew 8:2, a leper first worshiped Jesus and then asked for healing. Jesus said to him, *"I will, be thou clean"* (verse 3). Jesus never asked the man for faith. Why? Divine intervention had already stepped in, and it was time to praise God because of the provision for soundness.

Yes, we have the authority of Kingdom placement. And yes, we must now learn to walk in and live in the fullness of our God-given inheritance.

Shalom!

Righteous Decrees for Life

Father, by Your mercy, I receive the manifestation of a change of status now in the name of Jesus Christ!

Father, by the power of Your Word and Your Spirit, I command, "Favor, come! Prosperity, come! Breakthrough, come now in the name of Jesus Christ!"

Father, by Your Word in Isaiah 43:18-19, a mighty door of opportunity is opening to me in the days ahead. Help me to step boldly through it in Jesus' name!

CHAPTER 4

WALKING IN THE REALITY OF THE NEW COVENANT

Who hath delivered us from the power of darkness, and hath translated us into the kingdom of his dear Son.

Colossians 1:13

The New Covenant represents a translation from the carnal realm into the realm of the divine. It represents becoming invincible and indestructible in and through Christ. It shows us how to become one with God through the blood covenant.

The most powerful agreement ever conceived is a blood covenant. Only death can annul it. That was what happened between

Abraham and God, and that was also what happened between David and Jonathan.

When Jesus was sharing communion with His disciples, He said, *"Whoso eateth my flesh, and drinketh my blood, hath eternal life; and I will raise him up at the last day. ... He that eateth my flesh, and drinketh my blood, dwelleth in me, and I in him"* (John 6:54 and 56). Your covenant with God through Jesus Christ places you in the same class with Jesus.

The moment Abraham cut covenant with God, he became the friend of God, and God's ability, power, and glory also became Abraham's.

When Melchisedec met Abraham, he said, *"Blessed be Abram of the most high God"* (Genesis 14:19). That is what is imputed to you through redemption. The price Jesus paid on the cross of Calvary was to reconcile us back to God and make us sons and daughters of the Almighty. This assures us of an inheritance and sets us in place as heirs of the Father (see Romans 8:17).

Colossians 1:13 says, *"Who hath delivered us from the power of darkness."* The Kingdom you have been translated into is fortified with glory. Matthew 6:13 declares, *"Thine is the kingdom."*

The New Covenant did not start operating until Jesus put sin away, conquered Satan, rose from the dead, carried His blood to the Father as an atonement, and then sat down at the right hand of the Father. That was the birth of the new Kingdom He had said was *"at hand"* (Matthew 4:17). That Kingdom had now come. The power and glory of God was now here (see Matthew 26:27-29 and Acts 10:41).

The Word says that *"the kingdom of God is not in words, but in power"* (1 Corinthians 4:20). You are not to be tormented by the devil. Don't allow him to put fear in your heart. He is a liar. No matter how real what he says may seem, if it is not in the Word of God, it is a mirage, a lie.

> *And the great dragon was cast out, that old serpent, called the Devil,*

and Satan, which deceiveth the whole world: he was cast out into the Earth, and his angels were cast out with him.

Revelation 12:9

Each time the enemy tries to make you feel that God is very far away, your prayers will not be answered, or it's your sin that is causing this and that, tell him, "You missed it. My sin has been placed on Jesus, and now there is a covenant assuring that the divine presence of God is with me."

What most causes affliction in the Body of Christ is ignorance of the New Covenant. Hebrews 13:5 says, *"I will never leave thee, nor forsake thee."* That puts you in a place of honor, dignity, and security. That promise was made when Jesus was coming. Now He is here forever.

Under the New Covenant, we are taking the place of Jesus, ruling in His stead. Everything He ruled while He was here He has now put inside of us (see 1 John 4:17).

When Jesus met a blind man, He said to the man, " *As long as I am in the world, I am the light of the world"* (John 9:5). In other words, while He was here, He would shine His light on the men and women who sought Him. Then He restored the man's sight. Now we are the light of the world, and every form of shame and reproach has been destroyed.

Just as Jesus is the Light, you, too, are the light of the world, and this light cannot be overcome with darkness (see John 1:5). All you need is to renew your mind with the Word of God and shun all the suggestions that come from the evil one.

Because you know this truth, you can no longer remain silent when you see the devil oppressing other people. There is no fear in love. Step in, as the Holy Spirit is giving you direction, and knock the devil out, putting him in his place.

When you walk in darkness, you are walking in the realm of senses, and the devil takes advantage of that to intimidate you. You are now in the light, no longer in darkness. Therefore, darkness has no effect on you. The life in you produces light in you. This is called grace.

You cannot go into the world without light and win life's battles. But you are now the light of the world, and that means the darkness of this world is now in big trouble.

This is the light that Adam lost, and he then groped in darkness and was afflicted. Thorns and thistles were his food. The Earth was cursed because of Adam, and he was forced to live on that cursed Earth with darkness surrounding him. But Jesus came and made you and me the light, and there can be no sickness, no disease, no poverty, and no stagnation in the light.

In the New Covenant ratified by the blood of Jesus, you are perfected and sanctified, (see Hebrews 10:14), and Jesus has become the Shepherd of the entire new creation. He leads us by His Spirit to green pastures, and He restores and protects us. As David taught us in Psalm 23:5, even in the presence of our enemies, we are secure. This is not because we are smart, but because the Good Shepherd is always there to help us. When our great Shepherd is present, the adversary cannot even dare to speak.

Our covenant terms state that Jesus is our present help in any time of trouble (see Psalm 46:1). Isn't it about time that we enjoy our redemptive benefits in Christ?

Jesus is the light, and darkness cannot survive around Him. And, because His light is in me, I am also protected. By the authority in the name of Jesus Christ, Heaven is opened over my life, and Heaven's blessings now flow down to me unhindered.

As you can see, understanding our rights is crucial to our future. A proper under-standing will give us the ability to see what is available to us and enable us to lay hold of it, while others may be totally blind to its very existence.

If you cannot first see a thing, how can you take hold of it? And if you see it but do not know that it is yours, you will con-tinue to suffer lack. When you despise the Father's love and His covenant for your life, you may have excuses and reasons for every failure and every lapse, but the truth is that you are only robbing yourself.

The older brother of the prodigal son loved his father and worked for him, but he never really knew the depths of the father's love. By covenant, all that the father had was his, but he never really knew it.

The strength of our covenant is knowledge and understanding first of Who made the covenant with us. This releases our faith and gives us great confidence. Hebrews 11:6 declares: *"He that cometh to God must believe that he is ... ,"* not that He *was.* He still is, and He is still capable of creation, still capable of healing and delivering His people.

Hebrews 13:8 says correctly that Jesus is *"the same yesterday, and to day, and for ever."* He is the One who touched the mountain, and it smoked. Isaiah said that He weighs the mountains in scales (see Isaiah 40:12) and that nothing shall be impossible with Him. Our God is a covenant-keeping God.

The faith of Abraham was enhanced because he understood the significance of a covenant. It was a part of the culture of the day. He knew what God was capable of doing and that the covenant He had made with God committed God to do those things for him.

And it worked. All that God told Abraham He would do He did (see Genesis 17:4-7). God promised that kings would come forth from Abraham, and it happened. He told Abraham that he would be fruitful, and it came to pass. He spoke to Abraham of greatness, and the man achieved it.

Remember, however, that when God said all these things, there was nothing in the natural to show for it. They were just words, but they were God's words. It all must have seemed very strange and illusive to Abraham, but it came to pass, just as God had said it would.

In the same way, your greatness is now coming to pass in and through the name of Jesus Christ. God is committed to everything He has spoken to you, and nothing and no one can hinder it. All that is required is your cooperation, and you will see the mighty manifestation of God's power and glory in your daily life. Why? Because you are in covenant with God Almighty.

Men fail, but God's covenants never do. What God requires of you is to trust in the terms of the covenant (see Jeremiah 17:5-7).

One of the most powerful covenants God has cut with you and me is the covenant of peace. Ever since the fall of man, man has not known peace. Why? Because he walked away from it.

It was this lack of peace that brought all manner of frustration, fear, and worry to mankind. When Jesus came, He was different. He had perfect peace. In the midst of a storm, He was heard to say, *"Peace, be still!"* (Mark 4:39), and the storm obeyed. This shows us that a lack of peace is the cause of many of our storms.

When Jesus cut covenant with us, the covenant of peace, it did not signify an absence of storms, but rather power over such storms. Why? Because the Maker of all things would now be in the midst of the storm with us.

David sang:

> *Yea, though I walk through the valley of the shadow of death, I will fear no evil:*

*for thou art with me; thy rod and thy
staff they comfort me.*   Psalm 23:4

Death lost its power when Jesus came.
One of His names was to be Emmanuel,
God with us (see Matthew 1:23), and every
storm is calmed in His presence.

When you believe what God has spoken,
you are renewing covenant with Him. Every
word you believe becomes a covenant cut.
When you believe His Word concerning
healing, you are cutting a covenant of health
with God. When you believe His Word
concerning prosperity, then a covenant of
prosperity is cut with Him. Isaiah 9:6-7 tells
us that the government of Heaven came to
Earth to establish a covenant of peace, and
of *"the increase of his government and peace
there shall be no end."*

This peace is called *shalom.* The Hebrew
Lexicon describes *shalom* as "complete-
ness, safety, soundness (in body), welfare,
health, prosperity, peace, quiet, tranquility,
contentment, peace used of human rela-
tionships, peace with God especially in our

covenant relationship, and peace from war."
And God said there would be *"no end"* to
this kind of peace in our lives (see Isaiah
54:9-10).

You are safe now, you are sound now, and
you are prosperous now. Why? It's all part
of the covenant we have with Jesus. He has
done His part to establish the authenticity
of the covenant (see Jeremiah 33:20-21 and
25-26). Now, will you do your part?

The peace of God resides and abides with
you, if and when you release your faith into
the covenant. When Peter was told that he
would be killed the next day, he slept well
that night, for he had *"the peace of God, which
passeth all understanding"* (Philippians 4:7).
This is the peace that will set you above
every storm. This divine force will separate
you from the frustrations and limitations of
life. This is a gift from God that you must
accept. Jesus said:

> *Peace I leave with you, my peace I give
> to you: not as the world giveth.*
>
> John 14:27

This is the covenant God made with us through the blood of Jesus, and you can stand on that covenant and destroy all that the enemy has set up for you. It is time to rid yourself of sickness and diseases, worry and anxiety, by and through the blood of Jesus.

I have already been translated out of the kingdom of darkness and into the Kingdom of light (see Colossians 1:13). Therefore, I refuse to remain in chains any longer. Through my communion with Christ, I separate myself from all that is not for my benefit, and I do it in the mighty and matchless name of Jesus (see 2 Chronicles 15:11-19).

The blood which the children of Israel were instructed to put on the lintels of their houses was not just a painted decoration; it signified covenant. And something living had to be involved in its preparation.

Do you think any of the Israelites argued with God: "Why should I paint my doors with this blood?" Surely not. They were fully aware of the covenant they were making, and as a result, the angel of death that struck every Egyptian home could not come into the houses of the Israelites. This fact struck fear into the hearts of the Egyptians and caused them to be willing to give their wealth into the hands of these despised slaves, if for no other reason, than to get rid of them permanently.

The key to every freedom is the knowledge of the truth. Jesus said, *"Ye shall know the truth, and the truth shall make you free"* (John 8:32). Are you tired of sickness and disease? Learn the truth. Are you frustrated, depressed, or afraid? Learn the truth. Do you want to be free from fear and poverty? The knowledge of the truth is your answer.

David assured us:

He shall cover thee with his feathers, and under his wings shalt thou trust: his truth shall be thy shield and buckler.
Psalm 91:4

Jesus said in John 17:17, *"Sanctify them through thy truth: thy word is truth."* Truth separates you from every hardship and frustration. The reason "churchanity" and religion don't work is because they are centered on performance, piety, and penance, and not on the Truth. The truth is the guiding principle that makes things work.

Jesus said that we are in the world but *"not of the world"* (see John 17:14-16). There is a system designed to make you live an extraordinary life here on Earth. But it requires your understanding that God is a king who lives in the invisible Kingdom called Heaven, and that He wants His Kingdom to be duplicated here on Earth. Therefore, He created the Earth and then put His children here to manage it for Him.

Before they came here, God's children had been with Him (see Ephesians 1:4). God's intention was to rule, reign over, and dominate the Earth. Sadly, man "messed up" that deal by bowing down to an alien spirit, and was met with the spirit of death. In this way, he lost fellowship with God and lost confidence in himself and in God's perfect love. He said, *"I heard thy voice in the garden, and I was afraid"* (Genesis 3:10).

Thankfully, God stepped in with the concept of covenant, killed an innocent animal, and then used its blood as an atonement for man and his continuity. This concept was to reestablish man's confidence and his dominion over the Earth. He could now know that God was still there for him.

As we have seen, understanding the concepts of the covenant gives you total freedom from fear and builds strong faith in you. You cannot enjoy God until you know by experience that He is a God of covenant, that He knows the covenant He makes with you, and that He keeps His covenants.

Biblical covenants are divine agreements between God and man that commit God's integrity, ability, and power to the covenantee. This releases the mighty power of God, and defends you with who He is. This is our foundation for faith, boldness, and courage.

Living in covenant with God means relying solely on His integrity and His ability. He operates by covenant, and until you understand the concepts of His covenants, you will live in fear, especially when physical things don't go the way you expect them to. God has said:

My covenant will I not break nor alter
the thing that is gone out of my lips.
Psalm 89:34

In the Eastern cultures, where the Bible was written, covenants formed the basis of relationship and life. Until a covenant was cut, a person could not trust or rely on another. The faith of Abraham was based on God's covenant with him (see Genesis 17:2-11).

After Abraham had heard God's proposed covenant, he took a serious step and sealed it with the circumcision of his own flesh. This was his proof, a mark on him indicating that he was in covenant with God. And what was the result? God blessed Abraham *"in all things"* (Genesis 24:1). This was covenant at work.

From that moment on, God did nothing in the Earth without letting Abraham know about it. The evidence is that he forewarned Abraham of His intention to destroy Sodom and Gomorrah. Not surprisingly, Abraham was now daringly confident (see Romans 4:17-21 and Hebrews 11:17-19).

In the New Covenant of grace, physical circumcision is not required. God Himself has provided a blood sacrifice.

For by one offering he hath perfected for ever them that are sanctified.

Hebrews 10:14
(see also Galatians 6:15)

As you exercise faith in the Messiah and His covenant, you can go to bed in peace, knowing that He will surely keep you (see Colossians 2:10). For His part, God will release all His power and ability to back you up.

Under the Old Covenant, circumcision licensed you to be a partaker of the blessing. As long as you were born a Jew and circumcised, all other people on the Earth were inferior to you. You could not be afflicted nor defeated. Your victory was assured.

That was the confidence of Jonathan when he went to war against the Philistines (see Psalm 14:6). It was covenant that had brought the people of Israel out of Egypt, not their own efforts. They had no power and ability to fight the Egyptians, but *"God remembered his covenant with Abraham"* (Exodus 2:24). Therefore, He said, "Enough! You guys must get out of here, and I am going to punish Pharaoh for touching you."

There is an agreement between God the Father and Jesus. Jesus said, *"Of them which thou [Father] gavest me have I lost none"* (John 18:9) He said to us, *"Ye are the light of the world. A city that is set on an hill cannot be hid"* (Matthew 5:14). He promised to make us to *"sit together in heavenly places"* with Him (Ephesians 2:6). He made us *"more than conquerors"* (Romans 8:37). The covenant we have with God states that He will be with us *"always"* (Matthew 28:20) and assures us, *"If God be for us, who can be against us?"* (Romans 8:31). The covenant is in place, God is eternally committed to it, and the essence of the covenant is to display Heaven here on Earth through you and me.

The disciples understood what Jesus was saying when He declared, *"This is my blood of the new testament"* (Matthew 26:28). They knew it would commit Jesus' power and ability to remain with them and protect them for eternity. That was what increased their boldness and faith, and you and I are now operating under the same covenant.

When Peter and John came to the Beautiful Gate, they didn't have to beg God to heal the crippled man they met. They simply placed a demand on God, He responded, and the man was healed.

Under the New Covenant of grace, there is no room for regrets. Don't allow the enemy to frustrate you about your past. No, God makes all things to work together for your good. Even when you have "missed it," the Lord, the Messiah, steps in to work things out for you (see Romans 8:28). You no longer have to struggle to be justified. *"For it is God which worketh in you both to will and to do of his good pleasure"* (Philippians 2:13).

The New Covenant put God's own life into you. Jesus said, *"Whoso eateth my flesh, and drinketh my blood, hath eternal life; and I will raise him up at the last day"* (John 6:54).

The covenant is the source of our boldness. It eliminates fear completely, as you partner with God to rule the Earth. What cannot touch God also cannot touch you (see Colossians 3:3).

What did Zeresh say about Modecai? *"If Mordecai be of the seed of the Jews, before whom thou hast begun to fall, thou shalt not prevail against him, but shalt surely fall before him"* (Esther 6:13). That same night, Haman was hanged. You are in an even better covenant with God through Jesus Christ. Whatever seeks to hurt you will fail for your sake in the name of Jesus.

The Word of God is a book of covenant, but you will never enjoy the covenant until you know its terms. Let sickness become history in your life. Let lack never be your portion again forever. The days of your joy are here now in the name of Jesus Christ.

Covenant with God exempts you from frustration, limitations, and oppression from the devil and the world in general and puts you in the driver's seat for life. Why? Because God commits Himself to you and has vowed with His throne to get the work done, no matter what. It is God taking your place, standing with you, and defending you based on the agreement He made with you through Christ Jesus.

Abraham became a star to watch, but it happened by covenant, not by his own efforts. God took him from nothing and promoted him to a nation. In spite of every opposition, criticism, and economic frustration, the man excelled. The Lord said to him, *"I am thy shield, and thy exceeding great reward"* (Genesis 17:1). If God was Abraham's shield, whatever touched Abraham also touched God. God vowed to bless this man, no matter what, and He stood by that vow (see Hebrews 6:16-17).

Abraham didn't need to worry ever again. His covenant partner, the God of the

Universe, would take care of his business. As a result, unusual thing accompanied the life of this man.

Romans 4:13 says that God made Abraham *"the heir of the world."* Well, the world belonged to God, so Abraham inherited it. And according to the Scriptures, a covenant of God does not end with the covenantee. It affects his or her coming generations (see Genesis 17:7).

The covenant Abraham made with God affected Isaac. No one could cheat him or frustrate him, or God would step in and frustrate them (see Genesis 26:1-6 and 12-14). As a result, Isaac became the envy of his enemies. They tried everything, but could not stop him.

Even the economy bowed to Isaac. Even in the time of famine, the man prospered and went forward.

As Jacob grew up, the covenant of Abraham passed to him. When the economy in Canaan failed and people were begging to survive, Jacob gave money to his children to go buy food in Egypt. He was never poor.

When Joseph was in the house of Potiphar, the covenant of God located him, and he prospered there (even as a slave), to the extent that his master knew that God was with him (see Genesis 39:2-3).

It was this covenant that came upon Israel as a nation when they were in Egypt. None of the plagues that came upon the Egyptians came to Goshen. Why? Because God was in Goshen with His covenant people (see Genesis 47:27-28). These two distinct nationalities of people were there in the same country, and they were not all that far apart, but they experienced very different things. God made the distinction between them (see Exodus 2:23-25).

It was the covenant of God with Abraham that brought Jesus to Earth. God had said, *"And in thy seed shall all the nations of the earth be blessed"* (Genesis 22:18). It was all part of the covenant. Every seed of Abraham must be wealthy, strong, and healthy, and must live long and be anointed.

> *And if ye be Christ's, then are ye Abraham's seed, and heirs according to the promise.* Galatians 3:29

You are now in the same covenant because you belong to Jesus Christ. The New Covenant put you and me at the center of God's program (see Galatians 4:28).

Under the New Covenant, Jesus is the center of everything (see Ephesians 1:20-22 (MSG). There is no sacrifice required and no rituals to follow. The Scriptures only say, *"Believe on the Lord Jesus Christ, and thou shalt be saved, and thy household"* (Acts 16:31).

All the blessings of God reserved for humanity come to you when your attention is no longer on yourself, but on Jesus. The Bible says, *"They looked unto him, and were lightened: and their faces were not ashamed"* (Psalm 34:5). God is committed to you, as long as you keep your eyes on Jesus.

When you need healing, you activate the covenant of healing by looking at Jesus and not your doctor's report. When you need a breakthrough, prosperity, lifting, etc., your covenant is triggered by faith in Jesus Christ.

When Peter was sinking, he cried out, *"Lord, save me"* (Matthew 14:30), and He did (see verse 31). Cry out to Him today, refusing to be quiet about this, and your story will change now in the name of Jesus Christ.

Jesus said, *"And ought not this woman, being a daughter of Abraham, whom Satan hath bound, lo, these eighteen years, be loosed from this bond on the sabbath day? (Luke 13:16).* And the woman was loosed. Jesus was (and still is) the Covenant Executor.

By covenant, He is there with you now. No bondage will prosper today in the name of Jesus Christ. Heaven is open upon you, and the glory of the Lord is established over you now in Jesus' name.

The hindrance to full manifestation of your covenant benefits is a carnal mind-set, which frustrates the grace of God. We must all heed the words of the apostle Paul:

> *Casting down imaginations and every high thing that exalteth itself against the knowledge of God.*
> 2 Corinthians 10:5

The Word of God is the knowledge of God. It tells us what the covenant says. If what you are saying or hearing is contrary to the covenant, cast it aside right now. What is being said by others is not established, so don't release your faith into it. Stand on what God has said.

Yes, we are called to walk in the reality of the New Covenant, and therefore we must now learn to walk in and live in the fullness of our God-given inheritance.

Shalom!

Righteous Decrees for Life

Father, I refuse to be devalued by any force or situation in the name of Jesus Christ. In His name I receive all that the covenant affords me!

Father, I decree, by Your Living Word, that every limitation be removed from me and my life now in the name of Jesus Christ!

Father, I am the Body of Christ. No corruption is allowed here. No oppression, lack, or frustration is allowed here in the name of Jesus Christ!

CHAPTER 5

UNCOVERING THE SECRET OF VICTORY

In him was life; and the life was the light of men. And the light shineth in darkness; and the darkness comprehended it not. ... That was the true Light, which lighteth every man that cometh into the world.　　　John 1:4-5 and 9

If we can focus on the truths of the Word of God, there is enough power available for us to have a purposeful life here on Earth. You cannot use my present status and situation to judge me, for God has a plan for my life. He created this Earth with the intention of man ruling it, not Himself (see Psalm 115:16). Although He is the absolute power behind everything, man is His spokesperson:

> *And out of the ground the LORD God formed every beast of the field, and every fowl of the air; and brought them unto Adam to see what he would call them: and whatsoever Adam called every living creature, that was the name thereof. And Adam gave names to all cattle, and to the fowl of the air, and to every beast of the field.* Genesis 2:19-20

At that time, man did not know of any power except God's. The Bible does not indicate that God ever told Adam of any opposing or conflicting power. Adam apparently didn't know about Satan. All he knew was that he was here to subdue the Earth. That's all.

Oh, yes. God had said one more thing. "If you eat of the tree of knowledge of good and evil, you will surely die." In other words, "If you eat of the tree of the knowledge of good and evil, you will know what you are not supposed to know. You will be exposed to things that give you wrong information about you and about Me."

Death had already been defeated by God and thrown out of Heaven with Satan. He was the one with the power of death. God was saying, "If you eat the fruit, you will know who death is and how he operates because you will be taught how to die." Satan gained popularity through what he taught man, not what God had told him (see 1 Corinthians 8:4-6).

Man was not supposed to know evil at all. He and his wife were not just intended to be good; they were to be perfect, for that was his true nature and that of his Father.

God didn't want man to know about evil. Why? Because it would kill him. It would show him what had never been part of the divine plan.

As we know, Adam eventually ate the forbidden fruit, and his mind became terribly corrupted. Suddenly, he was misinformed. From that moment on, man became a slave to Satan and his cohorts because he kept hearing from the devil and not from God. Satan then became *"the god of this world"* (2 Corinthians 4:4) because man lost his place, became an alien, and was now unrighteous (see Romans 5:12 and 14).

The story changed completely when Jesus came to Earth. Through His sacrifice, He empowered man once again (see Luke 10:19 and Mark 16:17). When you accept Jesus and are born again, God uses the blood of His Son to purge your conscience from evil to serve the living God (see Hebrews 9:14).

Now you are not thinking about death, for the knowledge of the truth has taken over. You and I are no more under the influence of the devil. As far as you are concerned, he is a nonissue.

You have not just been rebranded; you are a totally new creation (see 2 Corinthians 5:17). God has made you righteous and put you in Christ, so that you can rule the Earth again. This time, it will not be with Satan-consciousness, but with God-consciousness.

Far too many times our thoughts empower Satan and not God because we keep listening to his lies based on what out natural senses can capture. God said:

> *For this purpose the Son of God was manifested, that he might destroy the works of the devil.* 1 John 3:8

If doors have closed to us, it is because we have allowed our carnal thinking to enable the devil to operate. In this way, he uses the God-given power we have to do his work. God has said that no one can shut a door that He has opened (see Revelation 3:7-8, so who is closing the doors? God's Word explains it this way:

> *Casting down imaginations and every high thing that exalteth itself against the knowledge of God.*
> 2 Corinthians 10:5

Divine plans don't oppose each other, and God is not the author of confusion. His plan is for you to live in a constant overflow because you have the life of God in you (see John 10:10, AMP). *"The God of Peace himself give you peace always by every means"* (2 Thessalonians 3:16).

When you are thinking about how to pay a bill or live in greater abundance, God is thinking about your Promise Land and how to clear obstacles out of your way to get you there. If you can learn to think like Him, you will have many more victories in life.

In order for man to operate in victory and blessing, God makes him righteous so that he can be in the same class as God Himself. That righteous standing was what was lost in the Fall.

Righteousness is a masterful thing. It puts us in the class of divinity (see Romans 5:17), makes ruling the Earth a reality, and frustrates the enemy's plans. It gives us confidence and boldness in the presence of the Father because we are able to approach Him with no sense of guilt from the past, as if our sin had never existed. We now live without the knowledge of sin. If you don't know you are righteous and have the same standing with God that Jesus has, how will you ever dominate like Him?

Righteousness comes by grace, through faith in the finished work of Jesus on the cross. It is not based on you, but on Him (see 2 Corinthians 5:21). It is a substitution. He who never committed anything sinful has been made sin, and we who never committed anything righteousness have been made the righteousness of God. We are now everything Jesus is to the Father.

This is where many people miss it. Under the Old Covenant, righteousness was by works. You had to earn it by your efforts, and people had to set tasks for themselves and constantly pressure themselves to be righteous.

Without righteousness, you cannot be blessed, and you cannot reign on Earth. It was unrighteousness that expelled Adam and Eve from the garden. But no man meets God's standard of righteous. *"All our righteousnesses are as filthy rags"* (Isaiah 64:6). Therefore, God provided righteousness Himself, not according to the Law, but according to His grace (see Isaiah 43:25).

This put us in a place of purity and total acceptance by God. And it is for this reason that we can now approach the throne of God with that consciousness: "I am the righteousness of God in Christ Jesus. Nothing can overpower me henceforth in the name of Jesus Christ."

Man was created as a creature of faith. Negative thoughts and doubt came after he ate the forbidden fruit and, therefore, had access to negative knowledge. It was that negative knowledge that created fear and doubt, and this lead to death.

What had happened? Man was hearing things that God was not saying and, therefore, he suddenly had wrong concepts about life. God had warned him not to eat the fruit of this tree. Now, his mind was corrupted, and the only remedy was to cast down every thought (see 2 Corinthians 10:3-5).

Through the complete work of Jesus on the cross, you are completely forgiven, you are completely righteous, and you now have the mind of Christ. BUT you must stop feeding on wrong fruits that bring doubt, fear, and death.

As Christians, no one is more righteous than another. However, some walk in their righteousness more than others (see Ephesians 2:8-9). Will you be one of these?

There is no fear in God's Kingdom, and fear is not a part of your nature either. God has not given us the spirit of fear but of love, power, and of sound mind (see 2 Timothy 1:7). We step into fear when we walk out of truth and into deception. If that happens to you, there is a remedy. Repent, declare your righteousness, and fill your mind with God's truths.

Jesus' understanding of righteousness was unique to the extent that even when He was in a storm, He was able to sleep. He was confident that the Father would do something to help Him. Because He was righteous, He knew He would never suffer (see Psalm 55:22, MSG). And, as the Father sent Jesus, He has sent us (see John 20:21).

Being the righteousness of God guarantees that you have certain rights in the Kingdom.

You have legal access to Kingdom properties, the right to sound health, to wealth, to favor, and to an unlimited supply of provision. That is why the Scriptures say: *"The righteous shall flourish like the palm tree; he shall grow like a cedar in Lebanon"* (Psalm 92:12).

The realm of the Spirit is the realm of perfection. Challenge every thought that attempts to pull you down and limit you, for you now carry everything that is in Christ Jesus (see 1 John 4:17). You may not have everything manifested already, but know that it is on its way to you even now.

Canaan was the Promised Land for the people of Israel. It signified the end of their labor and toiling. Jesus is our Promise Land, and I see what the Word says in Deuteronomy 11:10-12:

> *For the land, whither thou goest in to possess it, is not as the land of Egypt, from whence ye came out, where thou sowedst thy seed, and wateredst it with thy foot, as a garden of herbs: but the*

land, whither ye go to possess it, is a
land of hills and valleys, and drinketh
water of the rain of heaven: a land which
the LORD *thy God careth for: the eyes of*
the LORD *thy God are always upon it,*
from the beginning of the year even unto
the end of the year.

That is where we are now. We are perfectly loved and cherished, and we are the Bride of Christ. The problem is that not many think that way. Instead, we exalt our challenges, as if God were asleep and not caring for us constantly.

God never said that righteous people would not face challenges; He said that our challenges would not overtake us. In fact, He said that we would not need to fight at all. He would take over and fight for us (see Deuteronomy 9:1-3). That allows us to take charge of our circumstances.

It is nature that empowers the natural laws, but if you move above the natural, you will discover that what you think is an obstacle is not really there at all. The Law of Gravity exists only on the ground. When you get into space, it is no longer in effect. This means everything that exists naturally can be changed.

When Jesus came to Earth, He operated above the natural law. Even as His disciples looked at Him, He began ascending toward Heaven. That was above the natural law. He walked on water, and so did Peter. In the new creation, when we see obstacles, we simply move them or go around them by our righteous stand with God (see Romans 5:17 and Isaiah 54:17-18).

There are facts and issues, but they can always be changed. Your righteousness makes you a tool in the hand of the Almighty. You have access to everything. He said, *"The meek will he teach his ways"* (Psalm 25:9). Pray, "I am righteous in You, Lord. Teach me Your way in the name of Jesus Christ."

When you know you are the righteousness of God in Christ Jesus, nothing can stop you from creating your destiny and shining forth your light in this world. Jesus said, *"Then shall the righteous shine forth as the sun in the kingdom of their Father"* (Matthew 13:43).

Being righteousness-conscious allows the mighty power of God to flow through you without hindrance (see Philippians 2:13). You are not designed to live by your own devices. When you become His righteousness, He takes over for you.

I declare, by my righteous stand in Christ, "Help is coming for me in the days ahead!" I declare uncommon favor and promotion in the name of Jesus Christ. I move every natural law aside and decree by the power of the blood of Jesus, "Everything considered an obstacle or a limitation, be removed now from my path in the name of Jesus Christ!" This is your right too, my friend. Rejoice in Jesus' name.

Achieving righteousness under the Old Covenant demanded total obedience to the Law for the flow of the blessing, whereas, under the New Covenant, righteousness depends on faith in the finished work of Christ on the cross (see Deuteronomy 28:1-2, Acts 16:31 and Romans 3:21-24). It is not based on you and me anymore, but on Jesus Christ, the Son of the living God. Paul stated in Philippians 3:9, *"Not having my own righteousness, which is of the law, but that which is through the faith of Christ."*

Righteousness is important because it is the tool you need in order to reign in life (see Romans 5:17). Righteousness puts you on the same level as Christ. Righteousness speaks because it makes you fearless. There is no room for fear of failure in righteousness (see Romans 10:6-11). Because you are righteous, you are accepted, loved, favored, and cherished. You may now live with nothing wrong between you and your Father, God.

Everything was created to express something (see Psalm 19:1). The rose was created to express beauty, the lion was created to express bravery, and man was created to express divinity (see Genesis 1:26). You will always be needed because that is the reason for your creation (see Romans 8:19). That is why Jesus said, *"Ye are the salt of the earth .... Ye are the light of the world"* (Matthew 5:13-14). You have been placed at the center of the action.

DOING THE WORK OF CHRIST

When Jesus left the Earth, He put you here to continue His work, and the same forces that backed Him now back you (see John 14:12 and 20:21). This is not what any man planned; it is a result of the life of God resident in us.

The breath of life in man makes him invincible. John wrote that God *"hath given to us eternal life, and this life is in His Son"* (1 John 5:11). That is the force that produces results that are irresistible and unstoppable.

You cannot afford to fail. Life does not offer equal rewards for success or failure. It takes more effort to fail than to succeed, and God did not promise you failure. Jesus did not die to make failure available to you, but, rather, to abolish it (see 1 John 3:8).

As we have established, long ago Heaven planned what God meant for this Earth (see Revelation 4:11). Everything is for His pleasure, and you are the outlet of divine expression. Your desire to have joy, peace, and wealth is an expression of what God already made available through Christ, and the manifestation is through you.

The Scriptures say, *"He has planted eternity in the human heart"* (Ecclesiastes 3:11, NLT). You are able to achieve anything you wish in life because you came out of the most perfect material. It is called God (see Genesis 1:26-27).

God did not have any imperfections in Him, and always remember that you are a reflection of that same reality (see 1 John 1:7). It was wrong concepts that came from the enemy that brought any perversion in your life. So, think like God and not like the devil's suggestions.

I cannot imagine how failure and frustration could come to your life when God has already said, *"I am with you always"* (Matthew 28:20). We are only given one job as believers, and that is to reject what is not part of our makeup and accept what God put in us originally. If we are made in God's image and likeness, that is the most perfect material ever—pure and unique. This means all that we are looking for is already part of our makeup. 2 Corinthians 4:7 declares it.

Our environment, our experiences, and the enemy are the reasons for all failure, not because they are stronger, but because we listen to them, and they pollute our faith.

When the children of Israel were nearing any enemy city to conquer it, the Lord told them to destroy the city, its pagan altars, and all the people. Why? It was not that God hated those people. Not at all. It was because He did not want His people to be polluted and suffer oppression and death as a result.

Everything you learn apart from the Lord and His Kingdom ends in death. You are righteous in Christ Jesus. Learn how to operate your righteousness by:

1. Spending time in the Word of God (see Matthew 4:4).

2. Sharing the Word of God with others. (We call this evangelism.)

3. Meditating on your righteousness. Meditation brings strong imagination, and imagination produces a picture for the future.

4. Speaking the word of righteousness by faith.

We are not to experience failure caused by any force from Hell because we are the righteousness of God in Christ Jesus (see 2 Corinthians 5:21). All that He is has been transferred into our account. You are standing on the Earth as if it were Christ Himself standing here (see 1 Corinthians 12:27).

1 John 4:17 says *"As he is, so are we in this world."* You are not to be overpowered by any mortal or demonic power (see Luke 10:19). If the Head has overcome, the Body has also overcome. The challenge for the Church of today is ignorance of what Jesus did on the cross.

Forasmuch then as the children are partakers of flesh and blood, he also himself likewise took part of the same; that through death he might destroy him that had the power of death, that is, the devil.　　　　　Hebrews 2:14

Therefore, declare, "Satan, you are finished! Jesus fixed you for eternity!"

Righteousness brings you to a level of partnership with God in bringing His purpose to pass in the Earth realm. 1 Corinthians 3:9 declares, *"We are labourers together with God."* A holy and righteous God cannot partner with sinners. It is impossible. So He washes you and make you righteous like Himself. The mind cannot capture this truth. Only faith in the Word can understand it.

Your Partner and Helper is bigger and stronger than your every circumstance. He is the One about whom it is said, *"Casting all your care upon him; for he careth for you"* (1 Peter 5:7). The Word of God declares: *"Faithful is he that calleth you, who also will do it"* (1 Thessalonians 5:24). This is not just preaching; it is your life assignment. You are destined to be super-successful right now in and through Christ Jesus.

Through the redemption He offers, there is an empowerment that comes from God to you that enables you to prosper in everything you do. You are in Christ Jesus. This is just as Adam was in the garden before he sinned. You and I are now in Christ.

The following principles will help you realize your dreams:

1. **The force behind your life makes failure impossible.** No matter what confronts you in life, it is bound to be dissolved because God goes before you everywhere and in every moment, and mountains melt before Him (see Judges 5:5). He instructed the children of Israel:

> *Hear, O Israel: Thou art to pass over Jordan this day, to go in to possess nations greater and mightier than thyself, cities great and fenced up to heaven, a people great and tall, the children of the Anakims, whom thou knowest, and of*

whom thou hast heard say, Who can stand before the children of Anak! Understand therefore this day, that the LORD thy God is he which goeth over before thee; as a consuming fire he shall destroy them, and he shall bring them down before thy face: so shalt thou drive them out, and destroy them quickly, as the LORD hath said unto thee. Deuteronomy 9:1-3

God told Joshua:

Have not I commanded thee? Be strong and of a good courage; be not afraid, neither be thou dismayed: for the LORD thy God is with thee whithersoever thou goest. Joshua 1:9

Jesus needed to feed 5,000 people in a desert place (see Mark 6:35). Suddenly, the Bible says, there was grass there, and the people sat in the grass (see John 6:10). When God manifests His glory, every obstacle melts away. Just as the Father sent Jesus, He (Jesus) has sent you and me. It's time to see victory today in the name of Jesus Christ.

2. **Trust your word; it's the proof of your thought.** Your word comes from the depth of your thoughts. Never despise it because your word is connected to your spirit (see Matthew 12:35). Declare the word in faith, and it will go a long way toward your destiny.

Use your word against every seed planted by the enemy. You can dissipate every cloud of confusion around you by the word of faith that you declare.

Proverbs 23:7 says, *"As [a man] thinketh in his heart so is he."* Jesus said, *"Out of the abundance of the heart, the mouth speaketh"* (Matthew 12:34). So, speak boldly as the Lord brings the Word to your heart.

3. **Know that you are joined with God, and results are guaranteed (see 1 Corinthians 6:16-17).** There is nothing in you that attracts failure and affliction. That is all a borrowed idea from the kingdom

of darkness. You are joined with God, and you have the mind of Christ (see 1 Corinthians 2:16). Declare to yourself. "Going down is never an option for me. I cannot entertain fear, for it is not part of my being. I cannot accept discouragement from any source in the name of Jesus Christ. I am filled with the confident expectation of good always." In this way, you can reverse what is coming to your mind, never allowing yourself to become a victim of your circumstances.

You are breaking every barrier, for that is what you are made for. You are the righteousness of God in Christ Jesus. Declare, "I am not condemned; I am free."

The foundation for every confusion is separation from God. That was how death came. Restoration came through Jesus, and we are now reconnected, and all confusion must go. The Word of God says, *"Being reconciled, we shall be saved by his life"* (Romans 5:10). When the enemy comes to you with negative words, tell him, "I've been reconnected to God's righteousness."

Now, you cannot be separated from the life of God that is inside you. Neither can you be separated from the Kingdom of God that is planted in you. There is peace, joy, and righteousness in the Kingdom, and it's all within you now.

You are one with God, one with His Spirit, and the Spirit knows no boundaries and cannot be stopped. The Spirit cannot be frustrated, and it's everywhere ruling everything. David said, *"Whither shall I go from thy spirit? or whither shall I flee from thy presence?"* (Psalm 139:7). The Spirit of God is with you whereever you are, to help you and lead you, and to take down whatever stands in your way (see Isaiah 59:19). It's time to get to your destination now in Jesus' name.

Yes, we are uncovering the secret of victory, and, yes, we must now learn to walk in and live in the fullness of our God-given inheritance.

Shalom!

Righteous Decrees for Life

Father, I am now the righteousness of God in Christ Jesus. Every obstacle on my path, be removed now in the name of Jesus Christ!

Father, I am one with Your Spirit. Whatever is mine by redemption, I command you, "Come to me now in the name of Jesus Christ!"

Father, you always go before me according to Your Word. In the coming days, lead me into favor, divine connections, and divine appointments in the name of Jesus Christ!

CHAPTER 6

THE MASTER KEY TO RULERSHIP

For the gifts and calling of God are without repentance.   Romans 11:29

God does nothing on the Earth without a believer or believers praying. This is not to say that God lacks the ability to do anything and everything. However, He has bound Himself by this principle: mankind has been ordained to dominate the Earth and rule it.

God has all power and ability, but as we have established, He gave man the authority to act when it comes to issues of the Earth (see Genesis 1:26). Yes, man fell and forfeited his rights, but since God gave that responsibility to man, it is irrevocable.

Even the birth of Jesus Christ was ushered in by the prayers of righteous people. We know about at least two of them — Anna, the prophetess, and Simeon (see Luke 2:25-38). It takes your prayer to permit God to come into your territory and supernaturally impose His already-formed plan and bring it to fulfillment.

God has the power to take your life, but He does not have that authority. This is why He has said, *"Life and death are in the power of the tongue"* (Proverbs 18:21). God has power to prosper you, but He does not have the authority to do it. He has power to heal you, but He does not have the authority. It is your prayer that gives God the authority to use His power that is already available.

Prayer does not create things; prayer permits and enforces the manifestation of those things.

And I sought for a man among them, that should make up the hedge, and

stand in the gap before me for the land,
that I should not destroy it: but I found
none.   Ezekiel 22:30

Why was God seeking for a man? Because He needed authorization. As a biblical example, God was set on destroying Sodom and Gomorrah, but He did not do it without first consulting with Abraham (see Genesis 19:21-22).

There are things that provoke intelligent questions:

1. Observation
2. Knowledge
3. Results in the lives of people
4. Curiosity

The disciples of Jesus approached Him and said, *"Teach us to pray"* (Luke 11:1). People had been praying long before Jesus came to Earth. The people had heard the prayers of their forefathers, and the Pharisees and Sadducees also prayed. But this Man, Jesus, prayed with precision, accuracy, and power, and the results were there to prove it—wisdom, miracles, and signs and wonders. Therefore the disciples sought to learn to pray like Jesus prayed.

Prayer releases uncommon results. It is possible to pray and not see results—if you don't know *how* to pray. You may just be shouting and not praying at all. Real prayer uses the Word of God and applies biblical principles.

Jesus told His disciples not to pray *"as the hypocrites"* (Matthew 6:5). What did He mean by that? Hypocrites pray too, but there are no results to show for it. Prayer is not necessarily long, and it is never just a religious exercise. There is nothing wrong with long prayers, even hours of prayer, if the prayers being prayed are offered in faith and not with *"vain repetitions"* (Matthew 6:7).

Did you know that Muslims pray? Yes, they do. Buddhist pray too, Hindus pray, and so do Confucianists. The problem with their prayers is that they have no mediator, no intercessor, and no advocate. We have all of them in Christ.

You need to know that you cannot put pressure on God to answer your prayer. God is not just being informed when an issue starts. He knows the end from the beginning. Many times, in desperation, we cry out as if God doesn't know what is going on, and we need to let Him know. Therefore, we do all the talking, and then end our prayer with the words, "in Jesus' name."

Prayer must be a dialogue that involves two personalities—you and God. Listening and quietness is just as much a part of prayer as making petitions. He said, *"Be still, and know that I am God"* (Psalm 46:10).

We pray, "God, I need to pay this bill. I am behind, and if I don't get this bill paid by tomorrow, I am 'in the soup.' So, do it in Jesus' name." But that's not right. God already knows what I need. Therefore, I need to tell Him what His Word says, not what I feel about a given situation. Then I need to believe that what His Word says will happen for me.

The prayer of Jabez gets straight to the point. We are depending on the goodness of the God of Israel (see 1 Chronicles 4:10). Jabez called on God, saying, *"Oh that thou wouldest bless me indeed, and enlarge my coast, and that thine hand might be with me, and that thou wouldest keep me from evil, that it may not grieve me!"* And God granted his request.

Unfortunately, religion and tradition have taken over, and prayer has become a performance. Personal effort and a pursuit of legalism seem to be in vogue. For instance, many fasts are not inspired by the Holy Spirit at all. They come about because of emotion. Some think, "If I fast, I will be able to put pressure on God to act. At the very least, if He sees that I am nearly killing myself with this fast, He will answer me." Those who think this way simply don't know God. There is nothing you can do to impress Him above what Jesus has already done. In fact, what God recognizes most is your faith in His Son. Acts 16:31 says, *"Believe on the Lord Jesus, and thou shalt be saved, and thy house."*

Jesus made very clear the approach to prayer that gets Heaven's attention and approval (see Matthew 6:9-13). This was not meant as a prayer to memorize and repeat when we have a need. It is a model that shows us *how* to pray. It doesn't even contain the name of Jesus, and we know that is important to use when we pray.

Jesus began His model prayer with the words, *"Our Father."* The whole concept of prayer is empty and useless if we don't know God as our Father. Any meaningful dialog starts there.

Many, it seems, want to impress God by the effort they put into their prayers. It is easy to see that they are suffering and want God to act quickly on their behalf. Surely He must put their impassioned petition at the top of His list. But do they know Him?

Knowing God as a loving Father gives you confidence in prayer. He said, *"Your heavenly Father knoweth that ye have need of all these things"* (Matthew 6:32). The reason you think you need to put pressure on God in prayer is that you don't know Him well enough. Instead of trying to put pressure on God, try putting pressure on His Word.

As a loving Father, He understands your needs better than you understand them yourself.

It is religion that paints God differently from who He really is. It is a picture of a holy God, most powerful, who cannot be touched. Otherwise, you might die, as happened to Uzzah.

God's eyes are too pure for Him to behold sin, and that makes us afraid. Yes, that was true under the Law, but it is no longer true under grace. He said:

> *For I will be merciful to their unrighteousness, and their sins and their iniquities will I remember no more.*
>
> Hebrews 8:12

Yes, God is mighty, but He is also ever ready to step down to help sinners. Jesus demonstrated this by touching a leper, touching a prostitute, eating with publicans, entering and eating in the house of a sinner, and saving a thief. It is not who you are that frustrates Him; it is your unwillingness to accept who He is to you (see Isaiah 43:25-26).

God has redeemed you for His sake (see Psalm 44:26), and He loves you unconditionally. He is not mad at you. When you feel bad about things, He is also concerned, and He is there beside you to get those things straightened out.

Your heavenly Father knows how you feel. He has been there, so He can bear with you even when things don't seem to make sense (see Hebrews 2:18). He is your Daddy, so you don't have to manipulate Him in any way. When you call, He hears. If you have never trusted Him, it is, again, because you don't yet know Him (see Isaiah 65:24).

Jesus established your rights when He said:

And whatsoever ye shall ask in my name, that will I do, that the Father may be glorified in the Son. If ye shall ask any thing in my name, I will do it.

John 14:13-14

Just ask, He said, but most have not trusted the simplicity of this, thinking, instead, that they need to perform some ritual before being acceptable. But you are already acceptable to God in love.

The fact that God is our Father takes prayer to a whole new level. It is a pity when people shout at Him and still are not sure He has heard them. If you know He loves you, then you know He hears you. And if you know He hears you, then you have your answer (see 1 John 5:15). We know He hears us when we make our requests, and therefore, we also know that He will give us what we ask for.

Jesus did not just introduce the Father to us; He also showed us the Father's sovereignty and supremacy when He addressed Him as *"Our Father which art in heaven"* (Matthew 6:9). That's where Daddy is, and since nothing is lacking there in Heaven, you can be sure you will get what you need.

Daddy is in Heaven, and *"every good and every perfect gift is from above"* (James 1:17), not *from abroad*. Father God's position in Heaven makes Him an answer to every question.

It was *"the dew of heaven"* that Isaac bestowed upon Jacob that changed his life forever (see Genesis 27:39). This is because Heaven is the place of God's judgment and justice, the place of the final say. That is where Daddy dwells, so whatever comes from there is final.

Next, Jesus prayed, *"Hallowed be thy name"* (Matthew 6:9). It is your worship that shows you know how much the Father loves you. Because of His love, He is always there for you. And all He desires from you is your worship.

At the tomb of Lazarus, it was worship that turned the tables (see John 11:41-43), for Jesus prayed, *"Father, I thank you."* At the feeding of the five thousand, it was worship that made the difference. Jesus first *"gave thanks"* (John 6:11).

When Jesus prayed, He *"looked up to heaven"* (see Mark 6:41). Why? Because that's where Daddy is. And when Jesus prayed in this way, Daddy responded.

Daddy will respond to you too, for He is also your Daddy. Put the name of His Son in its proper place in your prayers, using "in Jesus' name," and see Heaven respond to you.

The Word says that God *"hath given us eternal life, and this life is in His Son"* (1 John 5:11). This is the force that produces results that are irresistible and unstoppable.

Jesus said, *"All things are possible to him that believeth"* (Mark 9:23). You may not understand everything God says, but be ready to believe everything He says. It is right believing that will give you a dominating force over all the powers of darkness.

I am in God's class of being, and therefore nothing created by Him can hinder, stop, or limit me. I and my Father are one. *"Greater is he that is in [me] that he that is in the world"* (1 John 4:4). Why should I be intimidated by lack, sickness, disease, or any other works of darkness.

In 1 Corinthians 3:21, the Word of God says, *"All things are yours."* Therefore, you cannot be denied anything ... unless you yourself do the denying.

Just as natural laws exist, and man is made to use the natural laws to his advantage, spiritual laws also exist and can be used to our advantage. Faith is a spiritual law that controls everything in the physical:

> *Where is boasting then? It is excluded. By what law? of works? Nay: but by the law of faith.* Romans 3:27

When you operate in the natural laws, you don't even have to pray about it. The response is there, and steps are taken. Try to stand on water, and you will sink. Be careful you don't drown. Jump from a great height, and you will be seriously injured. Stand on the Word of God, and you will win. Why? Because the Word of God is what faith uses to operate. It is the law of the Spirit realm.

Jesus said, *"The words that I speak unto you, they are spirit, and they are life"* (John 6:63). You are a victor now, never a victim. Get the Word into you, and declare it with your mouth. Then, give God praise for it, and see the heavens opened over you.

As God is absolute, there can be no opposing power (unless man makes the falsity of evil a god for himself). To show that you believe in only one power—God—and that there is no power or reality in evil, release your faith into what God says.

You attract what you fear. First of all, therefore, we must wipe out all fear. You must know that God protects your interests, and that the divine ideal must come out of every situation.

As we have shown, man was designed by God to take over the planet. That was the counsel of God (see Genesis 1:26). When man "messed up," God's program and His counsel did not change. In time, God found Abraham, and he was sent to take over (see Genesis 13:14-15). When Jesus found you and me, He sent us to take over (see Luke 10:19). In fact, John 4:38 says, *"Other men laboured, and ye are entered into their labours."* Today you are fulfilling the Word of the Lord in Jesus' name.

It takes prayer to fulfill that mandate. No prayer no victory! Why? Because prayer brings the manifestation of your dominion on Earth. You are calling God's attention to the issue. You can pray, "Life was not designed to be like this, because You, God, did not set it this way. Therefore, in the name of Jesus Christ, I demand a change." Never forget that you were sent here by God, and He is the owner of everything.

It is not just praying that brings results; it is praying correctly. The Bible says, *"Ye ask, and receive not, because ye ask amiss"* (James 4:3). Prayer can be an effort in futility if you are not getting the results you need and want. Prayer was meant to produce results.

You don't have to learn how to do miracles. If you learn how to pray correctly, miracles will follow. The disciples had seen Jesus do many miracles and were so convinced there was a secret to it that they asked Him, *"Teach us to pray"* (Luke 11:1). Prayer is what gives you access to the throne of God, where nothing is impossible (see Hebrews 4:16).

You cannot afford to be silent, for the enemy has vowed to make you miserable. Vow to take him out, and then do it in Jesus' name.

Matthew 13:24-28 shows that if something is bothering you, it is from the enemy. Pull out the tares. God's thoughts toward you are of peace. It is the enemy who sows the tares. Don't just stand back helplessly watching those tares grow. Uproot them now (see 1 Peter 5:8-9). *"Resist the devil, and he will flee from you"* (James 4:7). As the Message Bible states, shout a loud "NO" to the devil, and watch him *"make himself scarce"*:

> *So let God work his will in you. Yell a loud no to the Devil and watch him make himself scarce.*

The Passion Translation of the Bible says it this way:

> *So then, surrender to God. Stand up to the devil and resist him and he will turn and run away from you.*   James 4:7, TPT

Redemption puts you in a place of envy, and you can't help but be noticed (see Psalm 92:13-14), but there is one condition. You have a destiny of flourishing, not struggling, not sickness and disease, but it is your responsibility to resist the enemy and thus keeping him from stopping or hindering your destiny.

You can do this. You have the authority of the name of Jesus, and the enemy cannot take you out of your garden as he did to Adam and Eve. Never forget that the enemy will not scatter until you arise and take your place. That is how the Kingdom operates (see Psalm 68:1).

Don't allow the enemy to make your life look as if you have never been planned for. Get him out now in faith, as Jesus showed in Matthew 17:20-21 and John 14:30. If a thing is not from God, fight it with the name of Jesus Christ.

How do I know that something is not from God? *Every good and every perfect gift is from above, and cometh down from the Father of lights, with whom is no variableness, neither shadow of turning"* (James 1:17). The Lord will never tempt you with evil (see James 1:13) (see also Jeremiah 29:11 and John 10:10). There is no way you won't believe for it if you know it's there, and that God is interested in giving it to you.

But learn and follow proper prayer protocol. You are not to direct your prayer to Jesus, for example. You are to address the Father in the name of Jesus Christ.

What does this mean? It's simple. You have an account, but you can't get your money out of that account without a PIN number. The PIN number to your heavenly account is the name of Jesus (see John 16:23).

Prayer takes on a whole new feel when you know we are loved and well planned for. If you are full of worries and anxiety, these are clear indications that God is not in the picture. You can't be in control and God be in control at the same time.

The frustration many experience in prayer is that they want to deal with a situation and then let God step in. That is not the method the Word teaches (see 1 Peter 5:7). The moment we give a problem to God and walk away from it, the enemy brings it back to our minds. Whatever you do, don't take back the control of it. Refuse to have it. Stop neutralizing your prayers and then saying you've done your best when you clearly haven't. God's promise is:

When I cry unto thee, then shall mine enemies turn back: this I know; for God is for me. Psalm 56:9

According to James 5:13, if an affliction is to stop, you must pray. Why? When you live in the light, shadows disappear. It is not God who determines whether or not your prayer is answered; it's your faith (see Matthew 9:27-30 and Psalm 84:11).

Shall the prey be taken from the mighty, or the lawful captive delivered? But thus saith the LORD, Even the captives of the mighty shall be taken away, and the prey of the terrible shall be delivered: for I will contend with him that contendeth with thee, and I will save thy children. And I will feed them that oppress thee with their own flesh;

> *and they shall be drunken with their*
> *own blood, as with sweet wine: and*
> *all flesh shall know that I the* Lord
> *am thy Saviour and thy Redeemer,*
> *the mighty One of Jacob.*
>
> Isaiah 49:24-26

Yes, when you live in the light, shadows lose their place. Nothing is permitted to overshadow your glory, and anything that stands in the way must be removed in Jesus' name.

It is not information that brings trans-formation; it is understanding that establishes victory:

> *Give me understanding, and I shall*
> *live.* Psalm 119:144

> *Man that is in honour, and understan-*
> *deth not, is like the beasts that perish.*
>
> Psalm 49:20

God is not a man, so He cannot lie. When you believe God's Word, you have His commitment. He said, *"Heaven and earth shall pass away, but my words shall not pass away"* (Matthew 24:35). He watches over His Word to perform it (Jeremiah 1:12, AMP). Therefore, find the purpose of God and agree with Him, and that settles it. No crying! No begging! Just perfect peace!

This is called holiness. Holiness is oneness; it is agreement. That is why a double-minded person can never receive anything from God (see James 1:6-8). He is not holy.

When the Word says that you must not lie, your response must be, "Yes I will not lie. I am in agreement." That makes you holy. When the Word of God says that you must not commit adultery or fornication, your response must be, "Yes, I agree." Then, you are holy.

When God speaks to you by His Spirit and says, "Give Me the money that's in your pocket" or "Forgive that person who wronged you," instead of always asking why, ask what God's plan is and then agree with that plan.

God is a God of purpose. In fact, everything He created is for a purpose, and no matter what, that purpose must be fulfilled (see Isaiah 46:10). You won't need to sweat at all to see God's will performed. That was what made Mary pregnant. She said, *"Behold thy handmaid of the Lord; be it unto me according to thy word* [not according to my feelings or the prevailing reports]*"* (Luke 1:38). Peter said, *"Master, we have toiled all the night, and have taken nothing: nevertheless at thy word I will let down the net"* (Luke 5:5). God has purposed that you be above and not beneath, but it will only happen as you hearken to His voice.

Deuteronomy 28:1 shows that God's purpose is blessing, but He also tells us that we must make a choice (see Deuteronomy 30:19).

Adam was the first pattern man (see Genesis 1:26). God gave him dominion over the Earth and the ability to subdue it, but he "messed it up." Now Jesus is the Pattern Man for the new creation. He *"is the image of the invisible God"* (Colossians 1:15). All things were committed *"into his hand"* (John 3:35). *"It pleased the Father that in him should all fulness dwell"* (Colossians 1:19). Jesus loved God, and God loved Him and showed Him all that He did (see John 5:20, see also John 10:17). Jesus was one with God (see John 10:30).

But you and I are *"heirs of God and joint-heirs with Christ"* (Romans 8:17). We, too, are joined with Him and are one with Him. Therefore, we must be confident that God hears us and will answer our prayer, even as we are asking (see Isaiah 65:24).

The manifestation of our answer may sometimes be delayed and not come immediately, but God has heard, and He will answer. Therefore, we can celebrate in anticipation, knowing that He loves us and has saved us (see 1 Thessalonians 5:8-9, NLT).

This was the confidence Jesus had. He prayed, *"Father, I thank thee that thou hast heard me. And I knew that thou hearest me always"* (John 11:41-42). Lazarus was still in the grave, but Jesus was already starting to praise the Father for the miracle.

Truth limits the strength of the adversary. Why? Because it commits God's freedom.

You end every debate with the Word, not your opinion. Some physical evidence may be there to bring confusion, but we can't allow such confusion. If anything is not according to the Word of God, it must go.

You cannot have supernatural manifestations until you stop depending on what you see and feel. You cannot experience the impossible until you start seeing the invisible (see Hebrews 11:27). You don't need faith for what you've seen. If you believe you have two legs, that's not faith. Faith is for what is *not* seen (see Hebrews 11:1).

There was a personality in the anointing oil of the Old Testament called the Holy Spirit. We cannot see this Person, but the Word of God shows that He is there (see 1 Samuel 16:13 and Zechariah 4:6, AMP). So, when I apply the Holy Spirit to any issue, the results are guaranteed.

That was what brought creation into existence (see Genesis 1:1-3, see also Psalm 104:30). Everything invisible is made visible by faith in Jesus and this strengthens our faith and helps our understanding (Romans 1:20).

This is what James meant when he wrote:

Is any sick among you? let him call for the elders of the church; and let them pray over him, anointing him with oil in the name of the Lord: and the prayer of faith shall save the sick, and the Lord shall raise him up; and if he have committed sins, they shall be forgiven him.
                                        James 5:14-15

That's what happened to Mary:

The angel replied, "The Holy Spirit will come upon you, and the power of the Most High will overshadow you. So the baby to be born will be holy, and he will be called the Son of God."
                                        Luke 1:35, NLT

Yes, we have the master key to rulership, and, yes, we must now learn to walk in and live in the fullness of our God-given inheritance.

Shalom!

Righteous Decrees for Life

Father, I give You thanks because You are my Daddy! I am proud of that fact, and I glorify You in Jesus' name!

Father, I disallow every form of stagnation and limitation to my blessing! I command a release of my breakthrough now in the name of Jesus!

Father, I take right now every resource of Heaven provided for me by the finished work of Jesus on the cross! That includes health, prosperity, joy, peace, and soundness in the name of Jesus Christ!

CHAPTER 7

UNDERSTANDING THE NEW THING

And he that sat upon the throne said, Behold, I make all things new. And he said unto me, Write: for these words are true and faithful.   Revelation 21:5

Behold, I will do a new thing; now it shall spring forth; shall ye not know it? I will even make a way in the wilderness, and rivers in the desert.   Isaiah 43:19

New things have always been on God's agenda. From the beginning of time, everything was programmed to be new every single day. However, when people's minds get tied to the old, they cannot see and receive the new things God has promised. And, until you see a thing, you cannot receive it.

God's determination was to raise up a family on Earth to Himself through Christ. This speaks volumes to us. It was to be a family of results, a family of wonders, a family to be envied, a royal family, a family of new things.

The world had never seen this kind of family before, for this type of family starts with a new creation (see 2 Corinthians 5:17-18). You and I are directly connected to Heaven and were intended to make unusual waves on Earth. You are not common at all. Why? *"He who comes from [heaven] above is above all others"* (John 3:31, AMP). We are the children that have access to the bread and not the crumbs (see Mark 7:27-28). You are not here to suffer at all. Therefore, refuse to accept physical suffering as your portion in life.

The secret of our fruitfulness is that we are *"filled with all the fulness of God"* (Ephesians 3:19). Yes, to the brim. That makes it impossible for us not to produce results.

The way God sees things is completely different from the way man sees them. The good news is this: the way God views things is far greater and better than the way man sees them. God sees things from an eternal point of view, a loving point of view, a purposeful point of view. He said, *"Behold I will do a new thing, now it shall spring forth."* Receive it!

Every new thing that God manifests in our lives comes with a new mindset. You have to come on board and think the Bible way. You cannot have a new mindset and not turn to a new way of life. If you can't see it, you can't think it, and if you can't think it, you can't enjoy it.

God said, *"Behold I will do a new thing."* New things are great, but seeing them requires vision. If you don't have vision, all that God is set to do in your life may not be realized.

The spies from Israel saw themselves as a bunch of grasshoppers, while God saw them as a nation of kings and priests. The result was that they died in the wilderness without realizing God's plan because of their own blindness.

When God says, *"I will do a new thing,"* let's see what is on His mind and flow with it. His new things begin with *"I will make a way."*

I Will Make a Way

"I will make a way ..." The reason people become stagnated and depressed in life is because they can't see a way forward. To them, the door seems to be closed. In these circumstances, it takes a great deal of expectation from you to know that God will come through for you. You cannot be held bound by this situation any longer. A jealous God is coming for you now.

God said, *"I will make a way in the wilderness."* He is the Almighty. Therefore, making a way in difficult places is easy for Him (see Jeremiah 32:17). The space between where you now are and where you are going is called a wilderness, and the frustrating thing is that not everyone gets out of the wilderness. Many die there because they don't know the God of new things and how He operates.

The principles of God are there, and the testimony of God is proof that you are the next new thing. God is a specialist in new things, bringing new order and new results.

When God wanted to send John the Baptist into the world, He chose to do it through Elizabeth, a woman everyone knew to be barren (see Luke 1:36-37). Men said she was barren, but not God. Men said she was barren, but they were not God. The conclusion of others about you is wrong when you cling to God's Word. Whatever is said about you that is not from God will ultimately drop off of you, for God said, *"I will make a way."*

When unusual doors open for you, that is God making a way. In 2 Kings 6, one of the sons of the prophets, speaking of a borrowed axe that had fallen into the water, said to Elisha, *"Alas, master! for it was borrowed"* (verse 5). In other words, "We are done for! What shall we do now?"

Elisha, the man of God, knew that when a thing seems irretrievable, God steps in with a miracle, so he asked, *"Where fell it?"* (verse 6). Then the axe swam back to him. Whatever has been lost in your life is coming back, for the God of new things has not changed. He who said, *"I will make a way,"* is still making a way today.

What happens when God makes a way?

1. **When God makes a way, you experience supernatural favor (Genesis 6:7-8).** No matter what kills others, you are exempted. This is called favor. Even when the verdict has been pronounced, you will find favor. The qualification for Noah's favor was that he was a righteous man (see Genesis 7:1), but you are righteous too (see 2 Corinthians 5:21). Noah was in the ark, and nothing in that ark could hurt him. There were snakes, lions, and plenty of germs, but Noah survived it all.

The ark floated while every other living thing on the Earth died. You are in the living Ark, Jesus Christ, the Son of God. He

said, *"In me ye ... have peace"* (John 16:33).
No labor! No burden! Just total freedom!
When Noah got inside the ark, God shut
the door, and nothing and no one else
could get in. No evil could come in either.
You are saved inside the Ark, Jesus.

2. **When God makes a way, the enemy is
   disappointed.** Men cannot pull you down,
   no matter how much they try. Pharaoh
   said, "Now that they are shut up in the sea,
   let's go get them" (see Exodus 14:3-4), but
   he and all his army drowned. Every evil
   that targets your life is drowned today in
   the name of Jesus Christ.

   All the Jews in ancient Persia had been
   assigned to death, and the documents
   had been sealed by the kings signet.
   Then the God of Heaven and Earth
   stepped in. King Ahasuerus could not
   sleep (see Esther 6:1), and, as a result,
   the judgement was reversed. Every
   judgement against your destiny is also
   reversed today. God promised it in
   Isaiah 54:17:

No weapon that is formed against thee shall prosper; and every tongue that shall rise against thee in judgment thou shalt condemn. This is the heritage of the servants of the LORD, and their righteousness is of me, saith the LORD.

3. **When God makes a way, what kills others cannot kill you.** *"The LORD's portion is his people; Jacob is the lot of his inheritance"* (Deuteronomy 32:9). When there was darkness in Egypt, the children of Israel had light in their dwellings (see Exodus 10:23). When Paul was bitten by a deadly serpent, everyone expected him to swell up and die. But it didn't happen. Their expectations were dashed (see Acts 28:4-6). When God makes a way for you, people will change their minds about you in the name of Jesus Christ.

4. **When God makes a way, it means you cannot be stopped or hindered (see Isaiah 54:2-3 and Psalm 24:7-9).**

How to commit to God

1. **Believe His Word.** There is no room for new things if God's Word is not honored and put in its proper place. It was by the Word that things were created. Don't try to analyze it; just believe it.

Someone came to tell Jairus, *"Thy daughter is dead: why troublest thou the Master any further?"* (Mark 5:35). But Jesus said, *"Be not afraid, only believe"* (verse 36). Believe what? Jesus was saying, "I am here. I just healed the woman with the issue of blood. Your issue will be settled too."

Jesus told Mary, sister of Lazarus, *"Said I not unto thee, that, if thou wouldest believe, thou shouldest see the glory of God?"* (John 11:40). Believe what? Jesus had said, *"I am the resurrection, and the life"* (verse 25). He was saying, "Believe the Word now, and I will make a way." Thank You, Jesus. Make a way now, physically, spiritually, and financially. My way is made! Hallelujah!

2. **Declare His Word.** Every time you declare the Word, you settle that Word on Earth. The Word is settled in Heaven, waiting for your agreement on Earth. The rule is that with two or three witness the truth will be established (see 2 Corinthians 13:1). Heaven already established it, and you must agree with it now to be the second witness (see Mark 11:23). It was the agreement of Mary that brought the conception of Jesus. Agree with the Word, and see what God will do in your life.

3. **See the way God sees.** If you can't see what He sees, you cannot operate in His realm. The truth is: God speaks based on what He sees. He saw Abraham as a father of nations, but the man was past child-bearing age. Still, God said, *"A father of many nations have I made thee"* (Genesis 17:5). Even when he was unable to bear children, Abraham saw himself in the same light that God saw him. If you don't see what He sees, you will doubt Him and miss it.

God saw a Messiah in Mary, and Mary saw it too. She said, *"Be it unto me according to thy word"* (Luke 1:38). God saw kings in certain men in Israel, but they saw themselves as grasshoppers. What are you seeing? The Word of God is true. See it and own it.

4. **Be Kingdom minded and committed.** Membership is different from citizenship. Members are not always great. They are made up of cells, and cells die and are replaced. However, citizenship is eternal, and it's a responsibility. Be a citizen, and be responsible in the Kingdom. There is nothing you need in life that is not available to you now. All that is needed is your commitment to Kingdom business. All God wants to do with your destiny is subjective to this commitment (see Matthew 6:33).

The Lord is saying to you today, "I will establish you, and mighty doors, strange opportunities, will open to you. I will untie everyone that is held down, and there will be liberty everywhere, says the Lord."

His Word declares:

> *Instead of shame and dishonor,*
>   *you will enjoy a double share of honor.*
> *You will possess a double portion of prosperity in your land,*
>   *and everlasting joy will be yours.*
> Isaiah 61:7, NLT

God is digging into every area of life these days, and whatever is not glorifying Him will be removed in Jesus' name. The fire of God is set at every corner of concern, and this day they will be burned.

Why? Everything planted or growing in the wrong place must be removed. God said:

> *And in this mountain shall the LORD of hosts make unto all people a feast of fat things, a feast of wines on the lees, of fat things full of marrow, of wines on the lees well refined. And he will destroy in*

*this mountain the face of the covering
cast over all people, and the vail that is
spread over all nations. He will swallow
up death in victory; and the LORD God
will wipe away tears from off all faces;
and the rebuke of his people shall he take
away from off all the earth: for the LORD
hath spoken it.*   Isaiah 25:6-8

When you know the heart of Jesus Christ,
you can believe God for anything and know
there is no limitation for you in life. With all
that the disciples experienced, Jesus said to
them, *"Hitherto have ye asked nothing"* (John
16:24). It's time to start asking.

First John 3:9 teaches that we have God's
seed inside of us, and it germinates to produce a harvest that causes envy, not only in
physical results, but also in spiritual impact.
God's seed doesn't die. This brings the hope
and confidence that we are fully in charge
of life in Christ Jesus. As long as His seed is
inside of us, the future is secure.

It is true that Jesus Christ is coming back,
and we are awaiting His arrival, but the

sons and daughters of God must manifest first before the coming of our King (see Romans 8:19).

The Word is true, so stop believing the lies. They all end in delusion. God is true, and in Him there is no deceit.

We are putting on the glory of Heaven, manifesting His power now on the Earth. Nothing can stop the will of God in your life ... except you.

God's will is as powerful as His Person. It forms the foundation of His Kingdom (see Isaiah 55:11). God's will is that I do a new thing, and He is set to bring that to pass ... if I obey Him.

Spiritual laws are powerful and inde-structible, and they work ... if you work them. The same power that makes the child of the devil a child of God is avail-able to make all things new for you too. But see this: *"I will even make a way in the wilderness and rivers in the desert"* (Isaiah 43:19). God is ready to do new things.

WATER IN UNUSUAL PLACES

God will not just make a way; He will bring provision where there seems to be none, and He will quench your thirst.

God is not in the business of refurbishing; He loves to do new things. He fills you with the Holy Spirit and make you extraordinary.

If you are thirsty for God, He doesn't just have a little spring of water for you; He has rivers for you to swim in. It's up to you now, for God has already expressed His intention.

Great accomplishments are a possibility in Christ by the ministry of the Holy Spirit. The water of the Spirit poured into you will cause you to do extraordinary things (see John 7:37-39 and John 14:12). Our God makes everything new, offering fresh and new things from Heaven daily for the saints.

Teaming up with God by the help of the Holy Ghost is the key to walking in the realm of wonders. Jesus said, *"He [the Holy Spirit] will shew you things to come"* (John 16:13) and *"He shall glorify me"* (verse 14). You will never be without information when

175

God's Spirit is with you and in you. The King inside of you is crowned for reigning when the Holy Ghost comes over you.

You have now come to the end of thirst. To be thirsty is to be in need. From now on, you are to be fruitful. No more drought in your life.

You are also connected with many surprises. Can you see that now? You thrive when others are dying and struggling:

> *When men are cast down, then thou shalt say, There is lifting up; and he shall save the humble person.*
>
> Job 22:29

"He shall be like a tree planted by the rivers of water" (Psalm 1:3) Wherever this river flows, there is life (see Ezekiel 47:9).

You are becoming the envy of your world, and only you get that kind of reaction (see Genesis 26:12-14). You are refreshed, and you grow in new ideas. Here's how to make them flow:

HOW TO MAKE NEW IDEAS FLOW

1. **Walk in wisdom.** The end-time Church will be winning life's battles and conquering by practical application of the wisdom of God, which the world cannot comprehend (see Ephesians 3:10). This will draw the attention of the world to the Church (see Isaiah 2:2). *"Who are these that fly as a cloud, and as doves to their windows?"* (Isaiah 60:8). God's people will be high flyers. Why? Because God is bringing water to their deserts. The world is crying, but we are flying. It's called wisdom, and it comes by taking the Word of God as it is, while the world is busy analyzing and debating it.

   How can you explain the snake bite Paul suffered? All he did was shake the beast off into the fire, and he felt no harm. Those who witnessed this called him *"a god"* (Acts 28:6). Why? Because the life of God was in him.

   God said, *"By me kings reign and princes decree justice"* (Proverbs 8:15). If we are redeemed to be kings, wisdom is our identity.

Adam was ruling the Earth because his Father was the all-wise God. Even as a man, therefore, Adam had enough wisdom to rule.

"He that walketh with wise men shall be wise: but a companion of fools shall be destroyed" (Proverbs 13:20). Adam was walking with God, and the wisdom of God in him ruled the planet.

God's wisdom is His Word. That is why the presence of the Holy Spirit inside of you is the key to interpreting the Word. A wise man hears the Word and lives it. The resources of the Earth cannot be harnessed and put to use without the wisdom of God. How did Adam know that Eve was *"bone of [his] bones"* (Genesis 2:23)? It's called wisdom. And the magnitude of wisdom has been restored back to man through our Lord Jesus Christ. God made Jesus to us wisdom. Jesus is the Word of God. God's wisdom is God's equipment for supernatural manifestation.

2. **Be expectant.** Without expectation, faith is dead. Without expectation, there is no manifestation. Expectation is proof that you know God will show up (see Proverbs 23:18). It is a product of trust and positive anticipation.

Expectation increases your enthusiasm and confidence. If I were to tell you, "I will be giving out checks tomorrow afternoon about 2 pm," if you believed me, it would get your expectations up, and you would be contacting me about that time tomorrow.

God wants you to be expectant that your deserts have been turned into cities. He said, *"I will do a new thing now."* If you are expectant, then prepare for it like a pregnant woman prepares for her baby. When your expectations is in God, the enemy is doomed. Why? Because he can't stop it (see Psalm 62:5-6). If you know how big your Father is, you will expect anything and everything from Him.

Jesus showed us, in John 7:37-39, that He can't stand it when anyone is hungry or thirsty. Come to Him with great expectation. Change your posture and be expectant.

The crippled man at the Beautiful Gate was expectant, and he got more than he expected. He was made whole. Jesus is right there with you today. Be whole! The provision is there. Do you know it's for you? Take it now in Jesus' name. Don't do something just because other people are doing it. Do it with expectation.

3. **Believe in the ministry of the angels.** There are places God knows you can't get to, things you can't achieve on your own, so He has given you servants to get you to your Promise Land without a struggle (see Hebrews 1:14). The journey to your Canaan can be stressful, and there are giants on the way, but there is no giant that can stop the Angel of the Lord (see Psalm 103:20 and Exodus 23:20). Psalm 91:11-12 declares, *"For he shall give his angels charge over thee, to keep thee in all thy ways. They shall bear thee up in their hands, lest thou*

dash thy foot against a stone." These angels are always there to get the job done. They act on the Word of God on your behalf. Believe them and cooperate with them.

It was an impossible situation for a virgin to conceive and bear a child without a man, but the angel took the message to Mary and got the job done. Your angels are going to work on your behalf even now in Jesus' name.

FAITH FOR NEW THINGS

Everything that pertains to life and godliness has been purchased by Jesus Christ for you, but you will need faith to receive it. There is nothing in the physical realm that does not have its root in the realm of the spirit. The spirit realm is the manufacturing center, the production center for the physical realm. Tapping into the spiritual realm is called faith.

This realm is not accessible by the senses. In fact, there is no physical evidence that it exists.

Now faith is the assurance (title deed, confirmation) of things hoped for (divinely guaranteed), and the evidence of things not seen [the conviction of their reality—faith comprehends as fact what cannot be experienced by the physical senses].   Hebrews 11:1, AMP

All you need to see it is believe that God cannot lie. Then use it, because God is more real than your physical senses.

The struggle of life ends when faith comes into operation. Why? Because faith honors God, and whoever honors Him, He will honor. God honors faith.

The evidence of faith is the Word of God. If you see something in the Word, you can have it in your life (Mark 10:51-52). It was faith that gave the blind man his sight. Jesus came with sight, and faith received it from Him.

New things always follow when faith is alive. You don't have to be pitied by anybody. Walk in faith. Here's a simple approach: If the Lord says, "Do you believe I can do this?" answer, "Yes, Lord." If He says, "Do you believe I can heal you? Do you believe that by this time tomorrow, I can give you a miracle?" If your answer is yes, then be it unto you according to your faith.

Here are some steps to take to get your miracle:

STEPS TO LIVING A LIFE OF MIRACLES

1. **Know that God has not changed (Hebrews 11:6).** The foundation of faith is based on this truth. God is more current than you and I are. He is aware of what is going on now, and He has the power to fix it, just as He fixed the life of Abraham and the life of Daniel. No lion can swallow you because of who God is. He is still working today.

   But Jesus answered them, My Father worketh hitherto, and I work.

   John 5:17

2. **Know that God's love for you commits Him to bless you.** If you don't understand

God's dimension of love, it will be difficult for you to have faith in Him (see 1 John 4:8 and 16). We know and believe what the Bible says about love:

Love endures long and is patient and kind; love never is envious nor boils over with jealousy, is not boastful or vainglorious, does not display itself haughtily. It is not conceited (arrogant and inflated with pride); it is not rude (unmannerly) and does not act unbecomingly. Love (God's love in us) does not insist on its own rights or its own way, for it is not self-seeking; it is not touchy or fretful or resentful; it takes no account of the evil done to it [it pays no attention to a suffered wrong]. It does not rejoice at injustice and unrighteousness, but rejoices when right and truth prevail. Love bears up under anything and everything that comes, is ever ready to believe the best of every person, its hopes are fadeless under all circumstances, and it endures everything [without weakening].
1 Corinthians 13:4-7, AMPC

Love will do anything to get you blessed:

The LORD is compassionate and merciful,
* slow to get angry and filled with un-*
failing love.
He will not constantly accuse us,
* nor remain angry forever.*
He does not punish us for all our sins;
* he does not deal harshly with us, as*
we deserve.
For his unfailing love toward those who
fear him
* is as great as the height of the heavens*
above the earth.
He has removed our sins as far from us
* as the east is from the west.*
The LORD is like a father to his children,
* tender and compassionate to those*
who fear him.
For he knows how weak we are;
* he remembers we are only dust.*
Psalm 103:8-14, NLT

3. **Understand that the covenant of Abraham is a guarantee that new things must**

happen in your life too (see Genesis 17:5, Galatians 3:29 and 4:28).

4. **Never forget: something that has not yet changed or has not yet happened is not an indication that God has abandoned you.** A trial of your faith is not a denial of your blessing. In fact, it's just a preparation for a glorious future ... if you will not lose faith and quit. The Lord takes us *"through fire"* to bring us to *"a wealthy place"*:

> *For thou, O God, hast proved us: thou hast tried us, as silver is tried. Thou broughtest us into the net; thou laidst affliction upon our loins. Thou hast caused men to ride over our heads; we went through fire and through water: but thou broughtest us out into a wealthy place.*　　　Psalm 66:10-12

When you abandon yourself to God and His Word, it's no more faith; it's called trust. Job trusted God. He said:

Though he slay me, yet will I trust in him: but I will maintain mine own ways before him. Job 13:15

5. **Again, see the way God sees.** (see page 166).

Our redemption is the foundation for new things in our lives (2 Corinthians 5:17). In the Kingdom, nobody is permitted to fail and become obscure. No, as you are planted and watered, you will bear fruit. However, you must respond in order to see God's glory.

He spake also this parable; A certain man had a fig tree planted in his vine-yard; and he came and sought fruit thereon, and found none. Then said he unto the dresser of his vineyard, Behold, these three years I come seeking fruit on this fig tree, and find none: cut it down; why cumbereth it the ground? And he answering said unto him, Lord, let it

> *alone this year also, till I shall dig about it, and dung it: and if it bear fruit, well: and if not, then after that thou shalt cut it down.* Luke 13:6-9

When we experience the new birth, old things go. Holding fast to them reduces your impact. God is not mad at you. Even when you were bad, He loved you. Now that you are saved, He anoints you and employes you:

> *For we are labourers together with God: ye are God's husbandry, ye are God's building.* 1 Corinthians 3:9

Our lives are not structured to become stagnated. We are citizens of Heaven living on Earth, an example of divinity, an ambassador and representative of God on Earth. Our office is enviable.

If we are sent in the same way Jesus was sent, then we are living wonders. What happens here does not entangle us if we don't claim the citizenship of the Earth but of Heaven.

In times of trouble, the government of Heaven takes our case.

> *But the very hairs of your head are all numbered. Fear ye not therefore, ye are of more value than many sparrows.*
> Matthew 10:30-31

You are valued. Jesus said, *"I send you forth as sheep in the midst of wolves: be ye therefore wise as serpents, and harmless as doves"* (Matthew 10:16).

The manifestation of our redemption is all about:

1. **A new mindset, not religiosity.** As far as God is concerned, you are a victor:

> *But thanks be to God, which giveth us the victory through our Lord Jesus Christ.*   1 Corinthians 15:57

Satan is the victim, and this is true eternally. God means what He says and says what He means.

Nay, in all these things we are more than conquerors through him that loved us. Romans 8:37

You are a new creation in Christ Jesus (see 2 Corinthians 5:17). Your mind and your environment may deceive you, but faith in what God says always gives you the victory. That makes you reason like God and also behave like Him. We have God's nature now, His life, and His power.

Ye have not chosen me, but I have chosen you, and ordained you, that ye should go and bring forth fruit, and that your fruit should remain: that whatsoever ye shall ask of the Father in my name, he may give it you. John 15:16

Dominion means that you have a kingdom with a domain, and nothing is allowed to enter into your territory without your permission. Jesus said, *"Occupy till I come"* (Luke 19:13). The I-am-in-charge-here mindset is the secret of new things in the Kingdom (see Luke 10:19).

I am convinced that the reason for every oppression is ignorance. It kills faith and encourages fear. Faith, on the other hand, causes a revolution and serious intimidation in the camp of the enemy.

Thou preparest a table before me in the presence of mine enemies: thou anointest my head with oil; my cup runneth over. Psalm 23:5

For ye are bought with a price: therefore glorify God in your body, and in your spirit, which are God's.
1 Corinthians 6:20

You are valued, and because the cost determines the value, it took the life of God Himself to get you back. You have indeed been bought with a great price.

Satan is no longer the issue.

He that committeth sin is of the devil; for the devil sinneth from the beginning.

For this purpose the Son of God was manifested, that he might destroy the works of the devil. 1 John 3:8

If Satan is no longer the issue, then failure is under arrest. With sickness, disease, and premature death (including covid-19 cases), we see the captive holding his master in bondage. This ought not to be. Shake yourself from the dust, you captive daughter of Zion.

Awake, awake; put on thy strength, O Zion; put on thy beautiful garments, O Jerusalem, the holy city: for henceforth there shall no more come into thee the uncircumcised and the unclean. Shake thyself from the dust; arise, and sit down, O Jerusalem: loose thyself from the bands of thy neck, O captive daughter of Zion. Isaiah 52:1-2

Declare your emancipation now. "Enough, Satan, of sickness and depression!" (see

Isaiah 54:17). It is you who will disallow it, and then will God step in.

> *God forbid. How shall we, that are dead to sin, live any longer therein?*
> *For if we have been planted together in the likeness of his death, we shall be also in the likeness of his resurrection.*
> *Now if we be dead with Christ, we believe that we shall also live with him: knowing that Christ being raised from the dead dieth no more; death hath no more dominion over him.*   Romans 6:2, 5 and 8-9

There is no harassment here, not even from death. I was raised from the dead two thousand years ago with Jesus. Therefore, I cannot die again. I will only sleep when my assignment here on Earth is over.

The devil knows this, but your mind doesn't, so he uses what you don't know to imprison you. We are Jesus' testimony, the proof that He is alive. Signs and wonders are our identity:

And they, when they had heard that he was alive, and had been seen of her, believed not.

After that he appeared in another form unto two of them, as they walked, and went into the country. And they went and told it unto the residue: neither believed they them.

Afterward he appeared unto the eleven as they sat at meat, and upbraided them with their unbelief and hardness of heart, because they believed not them which had seen him after he was risen.

And he said unto them, Go ye into all the world, and preach the gospel to every creature. He that believeth and is baptized shall be saved; but he that believeth not shall be damned. And these signs shall follow them that believe; In my name shall they cast out devils; they shall speak with new tongues.

Mark 16:11-17

"They ... believed not." Acting the part of Christ physically must be our place which

manifests in signs and wonders. We are to speak like Him and act like Him. Why? Because we know that we share the throne of grace with Him. Therefore, we have full access. He said, *"Let us therefore come boldly"* (Hebrews 4:16). It's all yours, so don't be a coward. Failure is not an option. And this is God speaking, not a man.

Trapped within us, our spirit is from the omnipotent God and was intended to rule the Earth and dominate:

> *These things have I written unto you that believe on the name of the Son of God; that ye may know that ye have eternal life, and that ye may believe on the name of the Son of God.*   1 John 5:13

Our senses may be telling us something God did not say, because we cannot see yet what He said. But it is coming.

2. **The power of faith.** Faith begins when we see the authority of the Word of God,

as if Christ Himself is standing before us physically speaking to us. The Word of God does not contain life; it *is* life itself (see John 6:63). We are not trying to believe, and we are not praying for faith. We are believers, and we are in faith because we hear what He says and know that He is the Truth. What should we be trying to believe when we already have whatever He says we have?

Fear thou not; for I am with thee: be not dismayed; for I am thy God: I will strengthen thee; yea, I will help thee; yea, I will uphold thee with the right hand of my righteousness. Behold, all they that were incensed against thee shall be ashamed and confounded: they shall be as nothing; and they that strive with thee shall perish. Isaiah 41:10-11

Therefore let no man glory in men. For all things are yours; whether Paul, or Apollos, or Cephas, or the world, or life, or death, or things present, or things to come; all are yours; and ye are Christ's; and Christ is God's.

1 Corinthians 3:21-23

Far too many times we declare the faithfulness of Satan to do what he says he will do and declare the inability of God to do what He has promised. That has to be reversed.

Thou crownest the year with thy goodness; and thy paths drop fatness.

Psalm 65:11

The angel of the LORD encampeth round about them that fear him, and delivereth them. Psalm 34:7

And Jesus came and spake unto them, saying, All power is given unto me in heaven and in earth. Go ye therefore, and teach all nations, baptizing them in the name of the Father, and of the Son, and of the Holy Ghost: teaching them to observe all things whatsoever I have commanded you: and, lo,

I am with you alway, even unto the end of the world. Amen. Matthew 28:18-20

You cannot afford to be afraid of Satan and yet have no fear of God. *"He that cometh to God must believe that he is"* not He was (Hebrews 11:6). He is still doing wonders today for those who believe in and trust in Him, even when their circumstances do not seem to make sense.

God did not send the coronavirus. It is from the devil. You are of God, and therefore, you cannot fear what God Himself has already judged. It was not intended for you. God's Word says:

For he will rescue you from every trap
and protect you from deadly disease.
He will cover you with his feathers.
He will shelter you with his wings.
His faithful promises are your armor and protection.
Do not be afraid of the terrors of the night,

nor the arrow that flies in the day.
Do not dread the disease that stalks in
darkness,
nor the disaster that strikes at midday.
Though a thousand fall at your side,
though ten thousand are dying around
you,
these evils will not touch you.
Just open your eyes,
and see how the wicked are punished.

If you make the LORD your refuge,
if you make the Most High your shelter,
no evil will conquer you;
no plague will come near your home.
For he will order his angels
to protect you wherever you go.
They will hold you up with their hands
so you won't even hurt your foot on
a stone.
You will trample upon lions and cobras;
you will crush fierce lions and serpents
under your feet!
The LORD says, "I will rescue those who
love me.

I will protect those who trust in my name.
When they call on me, I will answer;
I will be with them in trouble.
I will rescue and honor them.
I will reward them with a long life
and give them my salvation."

Psalm 91:3-16, NLT

Be advised:

1. **I am free now.** Nothing will stop me again. I am sent as an instrument of honor, and nothing shall dishonor me in the name of Jesus Christ.

2. **I have life, victory, favor, blessing, joy, and abundance now in Jesus' name.** Who has the final say? Jehovah! Now that you know your value, it's time to start rating yourself by Heaven's standard. You have been *"bought with a price"*:

   Ye are bought with a price; be not ye the servants of men. 1 Corinthians 7:23

How much was paid for you? God's matchless Son:

> *Forasmuch as ye know that ye were not redeemed with corruptible things, as silver and gold, from your vain conversation received by tradition from your fathers; but with the precious blood of Christ, as of a lamb without blemish and without spot.* 1 Peter 1:18-19

The world may not value you because men don't yet know your worth. Getting your information from people who don't know you is a sacrilege. They will just confuse you and mold you to their standard and ratings.

The attention of Heaven is on you, since Jesus Christ paid the price for your redemption. Because of this, you and I become the most prized possessions of the Almighty. He said He would give people for our life:

> *Since thou wast precious in my sight, thou hast been honourable, and I have*

loved thee: therefore will I give men for thee, and people for thy life.

Isaiah 43:4

The One whom Heaven could not contain came down to reside within you. He is Emmanuel, God with us. See what the pagan Philistines said concerning Him:

And the Philistines were afraid, for they said, God is come into the camp. And they said, Woe unto us! for there hath not been such a thing heretofore. Woe unto us! who shall deliver us out of the hand of these mighty Gods? these are the Gods that smote the Egyptians with all the plagues in the wilderness.

1 Samuel 4:7-8

Again, Jesus said, *"I am with you always, even unto the end of the world"* (Matthew 28:20). That is enough strength in our weakness. The report from God is that Jesus came to give you life, and this life cannot be quenched or stopped by darkness.

But *"who hath believed our report"* (Isaiah 53:1), that slavery, oppression, poverty, and affliction has ended? *"The chastisement of our peace was upon him"* (Isaiah 53:5). It's done. I have peace now, so I take peace now.

The *Passion Translation* renders that verse this way:

> *But it was because of our rebellious deeds that he was pierced and because of our sins that he was crushed. He endured the punishment that made us completely whole, and in his wounding we found our healing.*
>
> Isaiah 53:5, TPT

Here are a couple more important things we must do:

1. **Understand the power of knowledge.** Your victory begins with knowledge. It is what you know that announces your destiny (see Hosea 4:6). New things don't come to you just because you are a Christian. They come because you have

the knowledge of the truth. The truth will come when you are willing for God to give you insight.

Discovering the power of the Word causes you to act on it. The Word is all God has for you to know about how He thinks about you and about His creative ability and what you are capable of doing in Christ. When He says, *"Behold, I will do a new thing"* (Isaiah 43:19), He is not asking for your faith as a believer; He's asking you to act. He is not just creating things by the Word; He oversees the Word, producing results.

> *Then said the LORD unto me, Thou hast well seen: for I will hasten my word to perform it.* Jeremiah 1:12

Doubting the Word is doubting the God who spoke it. God and His Word are one (see John 1:1). That Word changed Mary's life, it changed Joseph's life, and it will change your life too.

Agreement with God's Word releases favor into your life. When Mary said, *"Behold the handmaid of the Lord; be it unto me"* (Luke 1:38), she stopped explaining her situation and started acting on the Word. Too much explanation brings expiration.

When you start acting on the Word, it simplifies your life and brings you to total victory. Understand this: the Bible is God's revelation to man. It is what you can do that you have not attempted. It is the picture of your potential, which you have not yet released.

Yes, you can walk on water. You can turn your city around. God already approved it, and if you have never attempted it, it may be because you never saw yourself doing it. It is in you, and that is why God said it. Remove the limitations now, because His Word is true.

2. **Understand divine connectivity.** This new being, also called a new creation or a believer, was made in Heaven to manage the Earth.

The Father loveth the Son, and hath given all things into his hand. John 3:35

I in them, and thou in me, that they may be made perfect in one; and that the world may know that thou hast sent me, and hast loved them, as thou hast loved me. John 17:23

The new man was not created in dust but in Christ (see Ephesians 2:10). His is a complicated being that not even the devil can understand or interpret.

Whereby are given unto us exceeding great and precious promises: that by these ye might be partakers of the divine nature, having escaped the corruption that is in the world through lust.
2 Peter 1:4

Because the new man has a divine nature, he is connected to the throne room and is filled with the same Spirit that raised Jesus

Christ from the dead. Therefore, he is an oracle of God:

> *If any man speak, let him speak as the oracles of God; if any man minister, let him do it as of the ability which God giveth: that God in all things may be glorified through Jesus Christ, to whom be praise and dominion for ever and ever. Amen.*   1 Peter 4:11

But until the new man knows what is in himself, he may continue to live a life of slavery. He is destined to be fruitful in all things because he's attached to the vine and is well nourished by it. He just needs to know.

> *I am the vine, ye are the branches: He that abideth in me, and I in him, the same bringeth forth much fruit: for without me ye can do nothing.*   John 15:5

The new man is not subject to any devil because his seat has been changed and all things that bow to the Lord Jesus now bow to him. Why? Because he is now the Body of Christ.

Now ye are the body of Christ, and members in particular.

1 Corinthians 12:27

This position is based on divine connectivity, and it causes the new man to believe what Jesus has said about him (see Luke 10:19). This dynamic ability, which is resident in you, can be stifled by religion, tradition, and human experience. But, it is *"Christ in you"* (Colossians 1:27).

Therefore, you cannot be stopped. Christ cannot be in you and the Red Sea stop you. Obstacles must roll away for you just as easily as the stone rolled away from the entrance to Jesus' tomb. Your accusers must fall, just as Jesus' accusers fell down before Him.

He is there with you and in you even now. Loose the trapped ability in you in and through the name of Jesus. The ability of God is released as His name is invoked (see Mark 16:17-18).

Wherefore God also hath highly exalted him, and given him a name which is above every name: that at the name of Jesus every knee should bow, of things in heaven, and things in earth, and things under the earth; and that every tongue should confess that Jesus Christ is Lord, to the glory of God the Father.   Philippians 2:9-11

And whatsoever ye shall ask in my name, that will I do, that the Father may be glorified in the Son. If ye shall ask any thing in my name, I will do it.

John 14:13-14

Release the power now, and receive the new things that are awaiting you. In the days ahead, there will be miracles every-where, wonders everywhere, and all in the name of Jesus Christ. The God in us wants to work wonders through us even now.

For it is God which worketh in you both to will and to do of his good pleasure.

Philippians 2:13

Your connection with divinity is the foundation for the new things that will happen in your life, and that has already been established through Christ. That was His secret. He said, *"I and my Father are one"* (John 10:30). This caused Jesus to pray:

> *Neither pray I for these alone, but for them also which shall believe on me through their word; that they all may be one; as thou, Father, art in me, and I in thee, that they also may be one in us: that the world may believe that thou hast sent me.*　　John 17:20-21

"That they [this *they* includes you] *also may be one in us."* Yes, Lord. Yes, as I gain a greater understanding of the new things God wants to do in me, it opens doors in my life to greater blessings. And, yes, you and I must now learn to walk in and live in the fullness of our God-given inheritance.

Shalom!

Righteous Decrees for Life

Father, I give You thanks and praise for Your goodness and mercy over my life. You are gracious! Thank You for Your agenda of new things for my life in Jesus' name!

Father, in the name of Jesus Christ, I agree with You! New things, begin to manifest in my life—physically, spiritually, and financially!

Father, in the name of Jesus Christ, a great way is opened to me in the days ahead, in Jesus' name!

Father, in the name of Jesus Christ, every adversary of my new things is removed permanently now in Jesus' name!

CHAPTER 8

UNLOCKING THE FORCE OF UNLIMITED WONDERS

For by grace are ye saved through faith;
and that not of yourselves: it is the gift of
God: not of works, lest any man should
boast.   Ephesians 2:8-9

Living a life of wonders is complicated if you don't know what God has done for you in Christ Jesus. You have been totally restored to the Eden model. This is not something that you and I planned; it is the doing of God to achieve His purpose and dream for humanity. In Ephesians 2, Paul called it a work of grace.

Our calling is not a nomenclature. It is not a title. Our calling is a divine commission to power and rulership (see John 1:12). It is a calling to the demonstration of dominion over Satan, sickness, disease, lack, and death. We are deployed to show the superiority of Heaven over the Earth.

> *Then he called his twelve disciples together, and gave them power and authority over all devils, and to cure diseases. And he sent them to preach the kingdom of God, and to heal the sick. And he said unto them, Take nothing for your journey, neither staves, nor scrip, neither bread, neither money; neither have two coats apiece. And whatsoever house ye enter into, there abide, and thence depart. And whosoever will not receive you, when ye go out of that city, shake off the very dust from your feet for a testimony against them.* Luke 9:1-5
>
> *And he ordained twelve, that they should be with him, and that he might*

send them forth to preach, and to have power to heal sicknesses, and to cast out devils. Mark 3:14-15

Until you take the words of Jesus as an impartation of power, you will not see the demonstration of His glory.

And they were astonished at his doctrine: for his word was with power.
Luke 4:32

A child is conceived through the male and female gametes coming together. Nobody doubts that. The new creation is conceived by the joining of the Spirit of God and our spirit. In the process, there is a divine conception that takes place. Our body becomes a host of this new being. Many fail to recognize this because it is spiritually discerned:

But as many as received him, to them gave he power to become the sons of God, even to them that believe on his name:

> *which were born, not of blood, nor of the*
> *will of the flesh, nor of the will of man,*
> *but of God.* John 1:12-13

Jesus said it this way,

> *The wind bloweth where it listeth, and*
> *thou hearest the sound thereof, but*
> *canst not tell whence it cometh, and*
> *whither it goeth: so is every one that is*
> *born of the Spirit.* John 3:8

You are an airborne miracle, unstoppable and irresistible. That is why Isaiah 8:18 says:

> *Behold, I and the children whom the*
> *LORD hath given me are for signs and*
> *for wonders in Israel from the LORD of*
> *hosts, which dwelleth in mount Zion.*

Not just the Lord Himself, but also His *"children."* Therefore, every explanation for failure is a demonstration of ignorance.

David sang this revelation:

When I consider thy heavens, the work of thy fingers, the moon and the stars, which thou hast ordained; what is man, that thou art mindful of him? and the son of man, that thou visitest him? For thou hast made him a little lower than the angels, and hast crowned him with glory and honour. Thou madest him to have dominion over the works of thy hands; thou hast put all things under his feet. Psalm 8:3-6

This is the truth of what God created. You have become unstoppable by any force because you are a spirit. Anyone or anything that cannot stop Jesus also cannot stop you.

God wants Christ to reign on the Earth, for that is what will make Earth look like Heaven. This is what we are translated into when we are saved, to become creative wonders here on the Earth.

> *Therefore let no man glory in men. For all things are yours; whether Paul, or Apollos, or Cephas, or the world, or life, or death, or things present, or things to come; all are yours; and ye are Christ's; and Christ is God's.*
>
> 1 Corinthians 3:21-23

We are Christ's, and Christ is God's. That mentality brings you to a place of speaking to mountains, to cancer, and to the coronavirus, knowing that they must obey you.

This, of course, is not done in the flesh. It is done through your new creation, made in the image of Christ. Don't let that body of yours deceive you. There is a giant inside of you. Your spirit is stronger than your physical body, so don't judge yourself by what you see or feel. You have been introduced into a new world, a world where failure is not an option (see Colossians 1:13).

With your new birth, there are several important things you enjoy:

1. **Through the new birth, you are connected to the throne of grace (see Hebrews 4:16).** Everyone under the Old Covenant had to come through the high priest, and a sacrifice had to be made. Otherwise, death was the result. Nadab and Abihu, sons of Aaron, went into the presence of God without being invited, and they died. Now, however, you have the nature of God in you, and you are made righteous by the blood that washed you.

So, now, you may come boldly. God Himself certifies your competence to access His court. Therefore, go in by faith and take what you need. Nothing dies in that place ... ever.

> *And Moses laid up the rods before the Lord in the tabernacle of witness. And it came to pass, that on the morrow Moses went into the tabernacle of witness; and, behold, the rod of Aaron for the house of Levi was budded, and brought forth buds, and bloomed blossoms, and yielded almonds.* Numbers 17:7-8

The rod of Aaron budded and produced fruit overnight, and the same thing is happening to you now in Jesus' name. Coming into the presence of your Father guarantees undeniable fruitfulness. Because your spirit is reborn, the Spirit of the living God is poured into your spirit, and you can now know what God knows.

And because ye are sons, God hath sent forth the Spirit of his Son into your hearts, crying, Abba, Father. Wherefore thou art no more a servant, but a son; and if a son, then an heir of God through Christ.

Galatians 4:6-7

Remember, if you are sons, you will be heard. Father God said about Jesus, *"And lo a voice from heaven, saying, This is my beloved Son, in whom I am well pleased"* (Matthew 3:17), and *"While he yet spake, behold, a bright cloud overshadowed them: and behold a voice out of the cloud, which said, This is my beloved Son, in whom I am well pleased; hear ye him."* And He says the same of you.

2. **Through the new birth, you have access to divine instruction and direction.** The key to having wondrous results is having divine direction and guidance. Many have failed in life, not because they were sinning, but simply because they didn't know better.

> *The labour of the foolish wearieth every one of them, because he knoweth not how to go to the city.*
>
> Ecclesiastes 10:15

Your new birth gives you access to what the Spirit is saying because your spirit is connected to the Spirit of God inside of you.

> *For as many as are led by the Spirit of God, they are the sons of God. For ye have not received the spirit of bondage again to fear; but ye have received the Spirit of adoption, whereby we cry,*

Abba, Father. The Spirit itself beareth witness with our spirit, that we are the children of God. Romans 8:14-16

He that believeth on me, as the scripture hath said, out of his belly shall flow rivers of living water. (But this spake he of the Spirit, which they that believe on him should receive: for the Holy Ghost was not yet given; because that Jesus was not yet glorified.) John 7:38-39

Jesus said that rivers of living water would flow out from us. Job 32:8 declares:

But there is a spirit in man: and the inspiration of the Almighty giveth them understanding.

Proverbs says:

The spirit of man is the candle of the LORD, searching all the inward parts of the belly. Proverbs 20:27

There are ideas, concepts, and insights that God want to impart to you as an extension of His omnipotence for new things to manifest in your life. Your spirit can catch these, but your mind must also be ready to receive them.

3. **Through the new birth, you are connected with your potential.** You are born spiritually with so much virtue that it's impossible to lose your value (see 2 Corinthians 4:7). Everything created by God came out of parent materials that determine their function and potential. The fish came from water, and water is its strength. The animals came from the Earth, and the Earth sustains them. Although they live in the forests without fear, you cannot live there because you were not designed for that. The new creation man came from God and must be sustained by Him. The very nature of God is in him. Therefore He has all the attributes and character of God. Paul said it this way, *"I can do all things through Christ"* (Philippians 4:13). You cannot live

223

without results, for that is how you were wired to function.

We know that Cain was cursed:

> *When thou tillest the ground, it shall not henceforth yield unto thee her strength; a fugitive and a vagabond shalt thou be in the Earth. And Cain said unto the LORD, My punishment is greater than I can bear. ... And Cain knew his wife; and she conceived, and bare Enoch: and he builded a city, and called the name of the city, after the name of his son, Enoch.* Genesis 4:12-13 and 17

Even though Cain was cursed, however, he still had great potential. He built a city, sired a family and was blessed. Now it's your turn to break your limits. The nature of God was in Cain, and now that you are blessed, you must manifest wonders in the name of Jesus Christ (see John 14:12). It's time to start doing greater works and glorifying God in your life.

Many are born again but never experience wonders because Matthew 6:33 is not taken into consideration. You must seek God first, and then the wonders will manifest in Jesus' name.

We are redeemed as living wonders (see John 1:12). You cannot become a child of God and not walk in authority and power. That authority and power has been conferred on by your heavenly Father. By the Law of Creation, like begets like. This means that a dog can only give birth to a dog, a cat to a cat, and a bird to another bird. Each animal produces after its kind. God can only give birth to another god, and Acts 17:28 says,"*We are ... his offspring.*"

Speaking to things and getting results is our ordained position in Christ Jesus because everything is designed to obey us. Jesus said it this way:

> *For verily I say unto you, That whosoever shall say unto this mountain, Be thou removed, and be thou cast into the sea; and shall not doubt in his heart, but shall believe that those things*

225

which he saith shall come to pass; he shall have whatsoever he saith.

Mark 11:23

And the Lord said, If ye had faith as a grain of mustard seed, ye might say unto this sycamine tree, Be thou plucked up by the root, and be thou planted in the sea; and it should obey you. Luke 17:6

This explains what Adam did with all the animals in Genesis 2:19. Each animal became what he called it.

As you come into the royal family of God, you are vested with authority as a king to rule. Kings don't rule by "advice and consent" or human opinion. Kings rule by decree. God said:

Thou shalt also decree a thing, and it shall be established. Job 22:28

Where the word of the king is, there is power. Ecclesiastes 8:4

Revelation 5:9-10 also says that you are a king. God has made it so. However, God's view of kings is different from man's view.

> *And the* LORD *said unto Samuel, Hearken unto the voice of the people in all that they say unto thee: for they have not rejected thee, but they have rejected me, that I should not reign over them. According to all the works which they have done since the day that I brought them up out of Egypt even unto this day, wherewith they have forsaken me, and served other gods, so do they also unto thee. Now therefore hearken unto their voice: howbeit yet protest solemnly unto them, and shew them the manner of the king that shall reign over them.*
>
> *And Samuel told all the words of the* LORD *unto the people that asked of him a king. And he said, This will be the manner of the king that shall reign over you: he will take your sons, and appoint them for himself, for his chariots,*

and to be his horsemen; and some shall run before his chariots. And he will appoint him captains over thousands, and captains over fifties; and will set them to ear his ground, and to reap his harvest, and to make his instruments of war, and instruments of his chariots. And he will take your daughters to be confectionaries, and to be cooks, and to be bakers. And he will take your fields, and your vineyards, and your oliveyards, even the best of them, and give them to his servants. And he will take the tenth of your seed, and of your vineyards, and give to his officers, and to his servants. And he will take your menservants, and your maidservants, and your goodliest young men, and your asses, and put them to his work. He will take the tenth of your sheep: and ye shall be his servants. And ye shall cry out in that day because of your king which ye shall have chosen you; and the LORD will not hear you in that day.

Nevertheless the people refused to obey the voice of Samuel; and they said, Nay; but we will have a king over us.
1 Samuel 8:7-19

Your kingship will be very different from that of earthly kings.

The value God has placed on you is the reason He created you in His image. There is nothing that He did not put in you to be like Him. However, your continual manifestation of power and authority depends on your trust and complete obedience to His Word and your righteous lifestyle.

God told Adam and Eve, *"In the day that thou eatest thereof* [the fruit of the tree of knowledge of good and evil], *thou shalt surely die"* (Genesis 2:17). This means that death comes through disobeying the Word of God.

The devil, too, came to Adam and Eve and said just the opposite: *"Ye shall not surely die"* (Genesis 3:4). Unfortunately, Adam and Eve trusted the voice of the evil one, and they died.

The Word is still in effect. Jesus said, *"Behold, I give you power to tread on serpents and scorpions, and over all the power of the enemy: and nothing shall by any means hurt you"* (Luke 10:19). If you say, "I don't have it," you agree with the enemy who says you are too weak. God said, *"Whatsoever he doeth shall prosper"* (Psalm 1:3, see also Philippians 4:19). If you insist that nothing is working for you, it means that you have yielded your authority to the enemy and accepted death instead of life.

It's all about trust. Either it makes sense to you or it doesn't. The deterioration in the life of man is caused by his inability to agree with God and His Word (see Numbers 14:28).

Doubting the Word is saying that God has no integrity and that He does not mean what He says. That looks awkward on your part. Step out in faith now, for you have authority over every situation on Earth. This means you can dream big and obtain your dreams (see Colossians 3:12-13).

You have become the elect of God because of Jesus. It is the forgiveness of sin that changed your status and put authority on your lips. Therefore use it.

Receive these truths:

1. **You have a unique seat of power that rules over all things.** *"Since you have been raised to new life with Christ, set your sights on the realities of heaven, where Christ sits in the place of honor at God's right hand. ... And when Christ, who is your life, is revealed to the whole world, you will share in all his glory"* (Colossians 3:1 and 4, NLT). When Heaven's thoughts fill your mind, you will experience the manifestation of power and authority that makes you a wonder. You will enjoy a restoration to dignity and influence because Jesus reconnects you with the Father, along with all the privileges of the throne of God (see Ephesians 2:6).

   We are commissioned by God to represent Him and the government of Heaven here on the Earth. *"He that heareth you heareth me; and he that despiseth you despiseth me; and he that despiseth me despiseth him that sent me"* (Luke 10:16). Through what Jesus did on the cross, we now have intimacy with the Creator. But you must choose to believe it to see it happen (see 1 Corinthians 6:19-20, NLT).

2. **You have the Word of the living God (John 1:3-5, NLT).** God's Word is not just a message or an idea; it is a Person. It is a creative force. It is a tool to change situations in the Universe. There are things we no longer enjoy, not because that is what God intended, but because there came a perversion with the Fall. What makes things live is the life they have in them. Without this thing called *life*, they are dead. The Word of God puts life into everything it touches.

Since the perversion came, life is still there, but it works to the contrary. To stop that thing from living, you have to withdraw the life from it. That is why Father God gave you authority, and His Word is the tool for exercising it. For instance, we have authority over every virus through Christ Jesus.

When Daniel was in the lion's den, he survived, but was not because the lions were
not hungry. The Bible says he prayed, and
the Lord sent an angel to stop the mouth
of the lions (see Daniel 6:22). When the
apostle Paul was bitten by the poison-
ous snake on the island of Melita, he just
shook it off (see Acts 28:3-6, NLT). Now,
it's your turn to shake off the things that
are threatening you. You have authority
in Christ through the Word of God to
do these things. Meditate on that Word,
believe it, declare it, and see the glory of
God shine.

A centurion said to Jesus, *"Speak the
word only, and my servant shall be healed"*
(Matthew 8:8). What was he saying? He
was saying, "I know You, Jesus. You are
the Word of the living God." Jesus said,
*"As the father hath sent me, even so send I
you"* (John 20:21). Stop giving space to
the devil. You are the mouthpiece for
the Almighty here on Earth. He said we
would be *"a kingdom of priests"* unto Him
(Exodus 19:6). First Peter 2:9 says you are

"a royal priesthood." Speak now. That is your privilege, and you have the backing of Almighty God ... if you will only believe and act on it.

Cry out now! Remove things you don't want now in Jesus' name. For your husband or wife and your children, create something with your words. The Holy Spirit will do the rest. Amen!

The entry point into the covenant of God is success (see John 1:12). First John 5:4-5 says, *"For whatsoever is born of God overcometh the world: and this is the victory that overcometh the world, even our faith. Who is he that overcometh the world, but he that believeth that Jesus is the Son of God?"* (see also Galatians 3:29). This is the end of failure and frustration in your life in the name of Jesus Christ.

Equality with God was God's agenda for creating man. That was the original blueprint (see Genesis 1:26). In fact, the Bible says that we should be *"conformed to the image of His Son"* (Romans 8:29).

The first man is of the earth, earthy: the second man is the Lord from heaven. As is the earthy, such are they also that are earthy: and as is the heavenly, such are they also that are heavenly. And as we have borne the image of the earthy, we shall also bear the image of the heavenly.   1 Corinthians 15:47-49

If we bear the image of the earthly, we shall also bear the image of the heavenly. We are bearing the image of Jesus Christ. Jesus, who lived in the flesh and was proof that God could successfully be in man to operate as God. He was our Pattern (see John 20:21), and He took the form of man (see Philippians 2:7-8).

You are taking the form of man now, but you are God on the inside. You could not be equal with God without God's nature in you. Second Peter 1:4 says that we are partakers of His divine nature. How? Because we have become *"the righteousness of God"* (2 Corinthians 5:21). That is the pinnacle of all wonders in life.

The work of the blood of Jesus Christ is to wash us clean, as if sin had never been, and connect us back to God to live like Christ on Earth (see Ephesians 1:12-13). Now *"we have the mind of Christ"* (1 Corinthians 2:16). That exceptional mind gives us unparalleled thinking that can result in unusual success.

Salvation reveals the righteousness of God by making us new, like Adam and Eve before they sinned (see Romans 1:7 and 16-17). The restoration of man back to God is the foundation for success, and our continued fellowship with Him spells the end of failure.

God want us to enjoy the same fellowship He has with Jesus Christ (see 1 Corinthians 1:9). This involves talking to Him and also believing and acting on His Word.

The center of everything is Jesus Christ (see John 13:3). He has given us peace, joy, and fulfillment, just as the Father gave *"all things"* into His hands.

Satan knew Jesus Christ, nature knew Him, and the sea knew Him, and they all bowed before Him. Your righteousness in Christ will also make them all bow before you.

All of creation seemed to know what many believers don't yet know. Whatever Jesus Christ mastered, that is what we can master too.

Righteousness is a masterful thing. It is our gift from Jesus Christ, and He paid the price for us (see Romans 5:17). Enjoy it!

The moment you declare your righteousness, Satan loses all power over you. His weapons no longer work against you, and he can no longer overpower you. He knows that as you take the position of Jesus, he must move away from you. Why? Because righteousness is now your covering.

Arise, O LORD, into thy rest; thou, and the ark of thy strength. Let thy priests be clothed with righteousness; and let thy saints shout for joy.

Psalm 132:8-9
(See also Isaiah 61:10-11).

What Christ is now is what we are now (see 1 John 4:17), not what we should be or would be. Because this concept is not taught in our churches, many are living below the level of their privilege.

Does Jesus Christ have sin? Can He be sick? Can He lack anything? Then declare these same things for yourself.

Have you carefully considered the truth of 1 John 4:4?

Ye are of God, little children, and have overcome them: because greater is he that is in you, than he that is in the world.

If that is the Word of God (and it is), it means that we are superior to everything else on Earth. Your presence is intimidating to all the forces of darkness. God is there in you now, and, therefore, there is nothing you cannot overcome. The Greater One in you is superior to every potential foe.

This is the force that conquers cancer and infections, viruses, and high blood pressure.

It must all end in you now, for Jesus is re-claiming His property.

Your inheritance in Christ is shining and glowing. It is the foundation for your success in life (see Matthew 13:43). Therefore, start dreaming, and put your vision out there.

What would you do or say if you knew you could not fail, you could not be stopped, and you could not be successfully opposed? Then, do it! What would you say if you knew that what you said would actually come to pass? Then, say it now boldly, and believe it in Jesus' name (see James 5:16-17)!

Jesus is the Judge, He is the Justifier, and He has presented us to Himself without blemish, without wrinkle, and free of con-demnation in Christ (see Ephesians 5:27). That is the pinnacle of successful living. So, declare, "I am a living wonder!"

And the work of righteousness shall be peace; and the effect of righteous-ness quietness and assurance for ever. And my people shall dwell in a peaceable habitation, and in sure dwellings, and in quiet resting places; when it shall hail, coming down on the forest; and the city shall be low in a low place. Isaiah 32:17-19

The *New Living Translation* of the Bible says it this way:

And this righteousness will bring peace.
Yes, it will bring quietness and confidence forever.
My people will live in safety, quietly at home.
They will be at rest.
Even if the forest should be destroyed and the city torn down.
Isaiah 32:17-19, NLT

I am the righteousness of God in Christ Jesus. Therefore, sickness, drop off of me now. I regain my sight in Christ now.

Now, it's your turn. Talk to God, and let His Word and His works change you.

Declare something like: "I am the righteousness of God in Christ. Therefore, doors will open to me in the days ahead, and I will receive divine connections. I am the righteousness of God in Christ Jesus. Therefore, I have victory over sin, over bad habits, and over every weakness of the flesh."

Let the Spirit and your knowledge of the Word guide you.

Shalom!

Righteous Decrees for Life

I AM AN UNSTOPPABLE FORCE ON THE EARTH THROUGH CHRIST!

ALL THAT I SAY MUST COME TO PASS BECAUSE MY WORD CARRIES SPIRIT AND LIFE!

I WALK IN THE MIRACULOUS BECAUSE THE POWER THAT RAISED JESUS CHRIST FROM DEATH DWELLS IN ME NOW!

I AM BLESSED AND FAVORED!

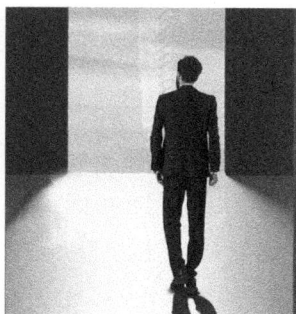

CHAPTER 9

WALKING IN THE MIRACULOUS

Today is not about healing and miracles; it's about Jesus Christ, the Son of God, and the proof that He is alive and is the same yesterday, today, and forever. The mysterious thing about it all is this: the world is confused and has never known the truth that Jesus is still here, alive and able. Unscrupulous people were paid to discredit the truth that He had risen from the dead (see Matthew 28:11-15). The fact that He works miracles and wonders proves that He is alive (see Acts 1:3). Because He is alive, there must be infallible proof of it.

I am sent by God to declare that He is indeed alive and is the Door to all that we need. He is present to prove it to us ... as we believe Him. Get yourself in line for blessings, for the battle over your destiny is finished (see Acts 10:38).

Miracles and healings are demonstrations of God's love and compassion for mankind. He cannot stand for any of His children to be in chains and lack the things they need (see Jeremiah 8:22). In the midst of chaos and death, He said, *"Let these go their way: that the saying might be fulfilled, which he spake, Of them which thou gavest me have I lost none"* (John 18:8-9).

The Bible says that a good shepherd lays down His life for the sheep (see John 10:11). Jesus, as the Good Shepherd, was *"moved with compassion"* for the needs of those He met.

> *But when he saw the multitudes, he was moved with compassion on them, because they fainted, and were scattered abroad, as sheep having no shepherd.*
> Matthew 9:36

Feeling compassion means that I cannot stand to see bad things happening to a person, especially when I have the power to change it. This was what caused Jesus' demonstration of compassion for the needs of people in His day. He was concerned for their material, spiritual, and emotional well-being and determined to change it.

He said they were like sheep without a shepherd. A shepherd makes sure his sheep have the proper pasture and never lack for anything (see Psalm 23:1-5).

Jesus was *"moved with compassion"* when He saw people suffering from sicknesses and afflictions:

> *And Jesus went forth, and saw a great multitude, and was moved with compassion toward them, and he healed their sick.* Matthew 14:14

Healing was a large part of Jesus' ministry. He could not pass the sick by. The good news is that Jesus is the same yesterday, today, and forever (see Hebrews 13:8).

He healed the sick in His day because He couldn't stand to see people suffering, and He hasn't changed.

> *And the inhabitant shall not say, I am sick: the people that dwell therein shall be forgiven their iniquity.* Isaiah 33:24

When there is compassion, the only requirement is faith to receive what Jesus is bringing to you. His *"compassions fail not"*:

> *It is of the Lord's mercies that we are not consumed, because his compassions fail not. They are new every morning: great is thy faithfulness.*
> Lamentations 3:22-23

No sickness can remain on you today because Jesus has not changed (see also John 6:2 and Mark 2:11).

Jesus had compassion on the fishermen of Galilee when He saw that they were not catching anything:

And he said unto them, Cast the net on the right side of the ship, and ye shall find. They cast therefore, and now they were not able to draw it for the multitude of fishes. John 21:6

He is indeed a God of compassion:

Therefore we ought to give the more earnest heed to the things which we have heard, lest at any time we should let them slip. For if the word spoken by angels was stedfast, and every transgression and disobedience received a just recompence of reward; how shall we escape, if we neglect so great salvation; which at the first began to be spoken by the LORD, and was confirmed unto us by them that heard him; God also bearing them witness, both with signs and wonders, and with divers miracles, and gifts of the Holy Ghost, according to his own will? Hebrews 2:1-4

But thou, O LORD, art a God full of compassion, and gracious, longsuffering, and plenteous in mercy and truth. Psalm 86:15

He hath made his wonderful works to be remembered: the Lord is gracious and full of compassion. Psalm 111:4

The Lord is gracious, and full of compassion; slow to anger, and of great mercy. The Lord is good to all: and his tender mercies are over all his works.
Psalm 145:8-9

That is why Jesus will do anything for you, even when you don't deserve it. He was moved with compassion everywhere He went. Therefore, miracles happened.

And Jesus, moved with compassion, put forth his hand, and touched him, and saith unto him, I will; be thou clean. And as soon as he had spoken, immediately the leprosy departed from him, and he was cleansed. Mark 1:41-42

We connect to Christ's compassion by faith through His name. His name contains His Person and is the proof that He is here and alive. His name carries His authority and power. He said we would do greater works through His name than He had done while here on the Earth (see John 14:12-14).

Why do the greater works come through Jesus' name? (see Philippians 2:8-11). Because the Lord is with us, and His name still has the same power. Just as He has not changed, neither has His name.

At the Beautiful Gate, this name worked wonders (see Acts 3:6-10). Whatever looks crippled in your life is receiving strength today in the name of Jesus Christ (see Acts 9:33-34).

The Lord who never changes is there with you, and His name that never changes is there as well. All you need to do is ask in that name. He is ready to get the job done for whoever calls on His name.

Whosoever shall call on the name of the Lord shall be saved. Acts 2:21

This salvation is still real today in Jesus' name. The life of Jesus is in the name. Take your salvation now by faith in Jesus' name.

You cannot afford to miss your greatness in the coming days. It has been predetermined and established upon God's divine covenant. As we have seen, when something is part of a covenant, you can rest in total conviction that it will be done. God said, *"I will never break my covenant with you"* (Judges 2:1). *"My covenant will I not break, nor alter the thing that is gone out of my lips"* (Psalm 89:34). The intention of God is to bless you, not to hurt you. If you live in fear and under pressure, it is because you don't yet know God's heart.

This was where the children of Israel missed it. They thought God had brought them into the wilderness to kill them and would give them a commandment to destroy them. The truth is that all He did was to bring them blessing (see Exodus 20:24).

God sent Jesus to Earth to bless you (see Acts 3:26). We have an Advocate, an attorney, who stands to plead our case and never loses a battle (see 1 John 2:1). The job of an attorney is to stand for you before a judge and get you out of your predicament. God is the Judge, and Jesus is your Attorney, and the good news is that He has never lost a case.

God is saying, "I want to bless you; that's why I sent you the Savior. The Savior came and said, 'I use the keys of David to open doors, and no man can shut them' " (see Revelation 3:7). Get these keys now and take charge."

Jesus told Peter, *"And I will give unto thee the keys of the kingdom of heaven: and whatsoever thou shalt bind on earth shall be bound in heaven: and whatsoever thou shalt loose on earth shall be loosed in heaven"* (Matthew 16:19). Knowing the keys, therefore, will give you access to greatness. Here are some of those keys:

1. **The key of consecration and commitment.** You will never need to scream and shout at any door if you are holding the key that opens it. Every man's glory is in

his story. When you know the story, you will walk in the glory.

David's heart of commitment to God's Kingdom knocked out every adversary standing in his way. He said, " *I had rather be a doorkeeper in the house of my God, than to dwell in the tents of wickedness*" (Psalm 84:10). *"One thing have I desired of the LORD, that will I seek after"* (Psalm 27:4). *"As the hart panteth after the water brooks, so panteth my soul after thee, O God. My soul thirsteth for God, for the living God"* (Psalm 42:1-2). God said that once He had made a vow, *"It shall be established for ever"* (Psalm 89:37). In fact, God said, *"I have found ... a man after mine own heart, which shall fulfill all my will"* (Acts 13:22). Jesus said, *"All these things do the gentiles seek: ..... But seek ye first the kingdom of God and his righteousness"* (Matthew 6:32-33). That's the key.

Psalm 92:13 says, *"Those that be planted in the house of the LORD shall flourish in the courts of our God."* Friend, where are you planted? That's the key.

The truth of 1 John 3:2-3 separates a person

for God: *"Beloved, now are we the sons of God, and it doth not yet appear what we shall be: but we know that, when he shall appear, we shall be like him; for we shall see him as he is. And every man that hath this hope in him purifieth himself, even as he is pure."* As the psalmist declared: *"My zeal hath consumed me"* (Psalm 119:139). Do you have this key today?

2. **The key of authority and power (Matthew 16:19).** The major strength of David was an understanding of God's divine presence with him always. No matter what confronted this man, he was very sure that the presence of God with him would bring an answer.

David sang, *"Though I walk through the valley of the shadow of death, I will fear no evil: for thou art with me; thy rod and thy staff they comfort me"* (Psalm 23:4). Everyone knows that the valley of the shadow of death was a terminal case, but God was there, and that made all the difference for David.

The purpose of God for every man on

the Earth is to rule and dominate in this world. David saw this. Every truth you know becomes a key in your hand. For instance, Psalm 8:4-6:

What is man, that thou art mindful of him? and the son of man, that thou visitest him? For thou hast made him a little lower than the angels, and hast crowned him with glory and honour. Thou madest him to have dominion over the works of thy hands; thou hast put all things under his feet.

This was the reason why everything bowed to David. He was able to say, *"Though an host should encamp against me, my heart shall not fear: though war should rise against me, in this will I be confident"* (Psalm 27:3). He had the key of authority and power through the divine presence. Jesus said, "I have the key of David, and nothing can stop me." He said, *"I and my Father are one"* (John 10:30). He said, *"He that hath seen me hath seen the Father"* (John

14:9). That was the key to the unstoppable results in Jesus' ministry. He said, *"Neither wilt thou suffer thine Holy One to see corruption"* (Acts 2:27).

And that key is with you now. Jesus said, *"I am with you always, even unto the end of the world"* (Matthew 28:20, see also Hebrews 13:5). God is with me. Love is with me, and love never fails.

3. **The key of death and Hades.** As we have seen, through the finished work of Jesus, death no longer has the final say over a believer. The death-dealing power of Satan was completely taken from him at the resurrection of our Lord Jesus. Because Jesus *"gave up the ghost"* (John 19:30), Satan lost the key.

What does Hebrews 2:14-15 mean when it says, *"that through death he might destroy ... the devil."* First Corinthians shows us the regrets of the powers of darkness. If they had known, *"they would not have crucified the Lord of glory"* (1 Corinthians 2:8, also see 1 Corinthians 15:54).

David saw this and used it. He sang, *"With long life I will satisfy him, and show him my salvation"* (Psalm 91:16). Seeing into the plan of redemption, he said, *"I shall not die, but live, and declare the works of the LORD"* (Psalm 118:17).

Jesus said, *"I am he that liveth, and was dead; and, behold, I am alive for evermore, Amen, and have the keys of hell and of death"* (Revelation 1:18). He is holding those key in your favor. So, use the keys. How? Stop speaking death. The Bible says, *"Death and life are in the power of the tongue"* (Proverbs 18:21).

Solomon was not just lucky; he had learned from his father (see Proverbs 1:8-9). We are moving forward today by the power and the anointing of the Holy Spirit in the name of Jesus Christ.

The seeds you sow have a voice, and they never remain silent. They speak even when you have forgotten and don't even pray about them (see 2 Kings 4:11-16). It was not the Shunamite's faith that saved her; it was her seed.

There is something about the tithe that projects into the destiny of your yet-unborn generations. Abraham did not meet Levi, but his tithes brought God into Levi's destiny. In fact, the Bible says, God Himself was Levi's inheritance (see Deuteronomy 10:9), but Levi was still in Abraham's loins when he paid his tithe (see Hebrews 7:9-10).

According to Hebrews 9:16-20, death is the guarantee that the benefactors now have access to their inheritance. A will is not mature until the death of the testator. That is why Moses would kill an animal and use its blood as proof of death for access. The blood of Jesus is proof that the inheritance is now mature for you and me. Therefore, we can now receive its benefits.

We have the most powerful team ever working with us in the New Covenant. Therefore, winning is assured. We are surrounded by myriads of angels who excel in strength and are our ministers. They make sure no stone or obstacles set by the enemy stops us. They always carry us in their hands lest we dash our feet against a stone.

Our heavenly Father Himself is the righteous Judge, Jesus is our Advocate, Intercessor, Mediator, and Savior. Therefore our justification is established. No matter how we have failed, we can go to the blood, repent, receive forgiveness, and, by the righteousness of God, become one with Him again instantly. Because of that, Satan and all his cohorts are in trouble.

You are now the righteousness of God in Christ Jesus. Therefore, Satan must take his hands off of you now in Jesus' name. He cannot lay claim to anything that Jesus has already paid for.

When we judge things by their physical appearance alone, we often miss the greater context. The greatest strength of a believer is to distinguish between what is eternal and what is temporal.

According to 2 Corinthians 4:18, things that are seen are temporal, and things that are not seen are eternal. The Bible declares that it (the Word of God) is eternal (see Isaiah 40:8). That is what controls the temporal. If something is seen or within the ability of the senses, the eternal Word of God can change it. That is what Jesus was saying in Revelation 3:8-9.

3. **The key of righteousness and grace.** One of the most powerful keys in the hand of Jesus is the key of righteousness (see Psalm 45:7). This is the ability to stand before God as if sin had never existed. This key opens any door at anytime because righteousness exalts and is a ruling force. You are accepted by God to do all you desire according to His will.

David understood that righteousness comes from God and not from our own efforts. He went into the Temple and ate the shewbread which was forbidden to anyone except the priests, and he escaped punishment for it. He said, *"Therefore the LORD hath recompensed me according to my righteousness; according to my cleanness in his eye sight"* (2 Samuel 22:25), not according to his own righteousness in his own sight. *"And in thy majesty ride prosperously because of truth and meekness and righteousness"* (Psalm 45:4). God confirmed David (see 1 Kings 14:8).

David's righteousness was not based on the Law, but on faith in the love of God. Actually, David violated the Law on multiple occasions. For instance, he was an adulterer (see 2 Samuel 11:4) and a murderer (see 2 Samuel 11:15). He was prideful (see 1 Chronicles 21:1 and 7-8), and a negligent father (see 1 Kings 1:6). His sins caused him great pain and anguish, as they did his entire family and nation.

We know that God was aware of David's sin, and He cannot lie. Still, David prospered. *"David also describeth the blessedness of the man, unto whom God imputeth righteousness without works"* (Romans 4:6)." We also know that God could not simply overlook the sins of David because of who David was. How, then, could God refer to David as someone who did only what was right? The answer lies in David's broken spirit (see Psalm 51:1-2 and Psalm 130:3-4). His connection to Jesus was the key to his righteousness (see Romans 5:17).

4. **The key of divine guidance and direction.** Beloved, success and breakthrough are part of our inheritance as children of God (see Deuteronomy 28:12-13 and Galatians 3:13-14), but how to attain that success is another thing. The Bible says, *"The labour of the foolish wearieth every one of them, because he knoweth not how to go to the city"* (Ecclesiastes 10:15). It takes divine direction to attain divine results.

The people of Israel knew they were going to the land flowing with milk and honey, but they were discouraged because they didn't know how to get there. To solve the problem, God led them through the wilderness (see Deuteronomy 32:9-10). One of the greatest privileges of the redeemed is to be led by the Lord in every situation. If you ask Him for guidance and you are willing to follow, Isaiah 48:17 says, *"I am the LORD thy God which teacheth thee to profit, which leadeth thee by the way thou shouldest go."*

Paul said in Romans 8:14, *"As many as are led of the Spirit of God are the sons of God."* How are we led by God? There is a witness within you. David asked, *"Shall I pursue?"* and God said, *"Pursue"* (1 Samuel 30:8). On another occasion, when David had asked, "Should I pursue?" God had said, "No." Being led and following that leading is crucial to our success.

Jesus said, *"I do nothing of myself; but as my Father hath taught me, I speak these things"* (John 8:28). You cannot afford to just jump into things. You are limited in knowledge about the future. *"There is a way that seemeth right to a man, but the end thereof are the ways of death"* (Proverbs 14:12). Ask God before you take a step. Pray in the Holy Ghost, and there will be an inspiration, a nudge. Then, follow that nudge by faith without wavering. If God can lead a donkey, you are much more qualified to be led by His Spirit.

5. **The key of faith.** Faith is not just religious language; it is Kingdom language. It is the currency that buys everything in the Kingdom of God. Jesus said, *"If thou canst believe, all things are possible to him that believeth"* (Mark 9:23). Faith is a conviction based on the Word of God. You cannot have faith if you don't know that the Almighty God who created all things is for you, and you can never have more faith in the things created than in the Creator Himself.

Hebrews 11:6 says, *"He that cometh to God must believe that he is ... ."* When you believe, you realize that His throne is the most powerful throne of authority in the Universe. From there, He does the things that please Him, and all that He does is to your favor. Why? Because He loves you. Knowing this, you cannot help but have faith.

God's Word is not a sermon, and it is not just an encouragement. No, it is His *will*. It contains His plans. It is an expression of His love for you. What you read in the

Scriptures is a love letter from your Dad, and it must come to pass, for the integrity of God is attached to it.

The key in the hand of David always works because it is based on faith in God's Word. David said, *"I had fainted, unless I had believed to see the goodness of the LORD in the land of the living"* (Psalm 27:13). Why? Because God said, *"My covenant will I not break, nor alter the thing that is gone out of my lips"* (Psalm 89:34). Nobody could stand against the power and the strength of Goliath without faith.

If you have faith but you never release it to God, you then release it into the ability of the devil because of the fears he has taught you. God gave you love, power, and a sound mind, but you learn fear by practice. If God says you have the keys, then you have them. Believe Him and start using them.

Remember, God said, *"I know thy works: ... thou hast a little strength, and hast kept my word, and hast not denied my name"* (Revelation 3:8). This means that even the people of the synagogue of Satan will bow to you. But you must first believe that He loves you.

The pressures of everyday life cause you to want to doubt God. Even the disciples said to Jesus, *"Carest thou not that we perish?"* (Mark 4:38). It was the pressures of the moment that caused them to doubt.

There, in Mark 4:38, the disciples called Jesus *Master*. In Matthew 8:25, they called Him *Lord*. In Luke 8:24, they said, *"Master master, we perish!" Master* is a word that comes before every situation. You may have neglected it because of pressure, but love has spoken, and love will stand by it. Jesus told Jairus, *"Fear not: believe only"* (Luke 8:50). Someone had come from his house and told him, *"Thy daughter is dead; trouble not the Master"* (Luke 8:49). Bad news must not move us when Jesus is with us.

As we noted before, when Jesus heard about the sickness of Lazarus, He said, *"This sickness is not unto death"* (John 11:4). Still, the family and friends buried

Lazarus and sealed up his tomb. Jesus said it's *"not unto death,"* even though Martha said, *"By this time he stinketh"* (John 11:49). Even though Jesus had said, *"This sickness is not unto death,"* everyone in Bethany was weeping and making funeral arrangements.

God's Word declares that Jesus has redeemed us from the curse of the Law. His Word declares, *"by whose stripes ye were healed"* (1 Peter 2:24). It says, *"Though he was rich, yet for your sakes he became poor, that ye through his poverty might be rich"* (2 Corinthians 8:9). It says, *"I had believed to see the goodness of the Lord in the land of the living"* (Psalm 27:13). It says, *"Ask, and it shall be given you"* (Matthew 7:7). Life is not over yet, and things are changing for those who believe.

The Lord cannot give you more than your ability to receive, even though the supply end is never lacking. Remember, the Bible says the work was *"finished from the foundation of the world"* (Hebrews 4:3), but the receiving of the finished work is a daily affair that we must achieve by faith.

There is a mystery behind the veil that was torn from top to bottom at the resurrection of Jesus. It had not been designed by Moses. God gave him specific instructions for its design.

Behind the veil was an image of the cherubim of glory. And there was something all Israel waited for every time the high priest went inside. He never went there alone. He always went in with the blood, after the offering and sacrifices had been made. And when he came out, he never came out alone. He always came with a blessing for the people (see Numbers 6:22-27).

When the high priest came out, everyone was there waiting for their blessing. It was not because of the priest, but because of the presence of the Lord that resided in the Most Holy Place. It was not the man; it was the Lord that rested upon the man. After the resurrection of Jesus, the priesthood changed. It was no more from Aaron and his descendants. When the Law changed, so did the operation of it. Even the tribe had changed. Now a new Priest,

267

One after the order of Melchizedek, came. His coming was not by the Law, but by appointment (see Hebrews 7:17-21).

There was nothing Abraham did to bring Melchizedek and his blessing to himself. In fact, he had not yet brought Isaac to the altar, nor had he circumcised himself (see Genesis 14:18-).

Jesus died at the hands of Roman soldiers, but they were just executing the orders of the Jewish high priest. Instead of Jesus coming out of the Holy of Hollies to bless the people and ask them to come back the next year, He removed the veil completely. Now the blessing was available to everyone who believed, and the heavens were no more closed against us. We, therefore, now have access to God's throne.

The Old Testament saints prayed for the heavens to be opened for them. Now, however, the heavens remain open because Jesus opened them. All we need to do is command the release of our portion. The priesthood of Jesus was after the order of Melchizedek, not after the order

of Aaron. How did Melchizedek operate? (see Genesis 14:18-21). He blessed
Abraham and gave him the key to Heaven
and Earth. Romans 4:17 shows that it was
not because Abraham paid tithes; it was
grace in action. The tithe was just the proof
that Abraham was blessed.

If you are not tithing, you are telling God
that He has not blessed you, that He lied,
and, therefore, you are refusing to honor
Him (see Revelation 3:6-7).

To close the heavens, you would have to
change the priesthood again and the Law.
That would be impossible because Jesus
is the High Priest forever after the order
of Melchizedek. He blesses and keeps on
blessing. Your access to everything in the
Kingdom is through Jesus. He has the key
(see Philippians 2:8-10 and 1 Peter 3:22).

Now it's our turn to reign on the Earth.
This great High Priest has entered into
the heavens, and with His sacrifice He has
appeased the Father. Therefore, we can
now come boldly, based on Him and not
on ourselves (see Hebrews 4:14-16, NLT).

It is important to note that opening the heavens involved the use of relevant keys. The Word of God says that I have the keys of David, so that when I open, no one can close, and when I close, no one can open. Keys speak of authority, dominion, and power. Having keys is an indication that you are in charge of things. The key of David can be used by anyone of faith, and Jesus said I have that key right here and right now.

6. **The key of the covenant.** Covenant is the bedrock of our confidence in God. Covenant is a divine agreement between God and man, with an oath based on established terms and principles. God is a covenant-keeping God, and because of the covenant, it is a surety that God Almighty is committed to us. This was a key in the hand of David that opened to him doors of victory and triumph.

When the armies of Israel were facing Goliath, it was like facing an insurmountable object. To those military men, it looked like the end. This huge man was a vicious warrior, and his sheer size was intimidating. He insulted the armies of Israel and called God names, and he did this for forty straight days. When it seemed to the men of Israel that God would never respond, they got very depressed ... that is until the man with the keys showed up.

It was the young David, and when he saw what was happening, he said *"Who is this uncircumcised Philistines* [a man with no covenant], *that he should defy the armies of the living God?"* (1 Samuel 17:26). Then, to Goliath, he said, *"I will smite thee, and take thine head from thee"* (verse 46). All that Israel needed was in the camp, but the door had been closed by Goliath. David opened it by invoking the covenant, and he knew that this door could be kept open continually by using the key of covenant (see Jeremiah 23:4-6 and Psalm 89:35-37). In time, the Messiah came through the lineage of David by covenant. When He had stepped into His position, He said, *"I and my Father are one"* (John 10:30).This same covenant is available to you now in and through Christ. Use the key of covenant. For instance, Mark 16:17-18 is a covenant you can count on.

7. **The key of the anointing.** The anointing of the Holy Spirit is the divine enablement of God to cause you to do things you could not do in your natural ability. It is the supernatural hand of God upon your life to cause you to excel beyond any limits. The anointing will enable you to raise your children supernaturally, to manage your health supernaturally, and to manage your business and your home supernaturally.

When the anointing came upon Samson, he was able to kill a lion with his bare hands. When it came upon Jehu, he was able to kill the wicked Queen Jezebel. When it came upon Elijah, he outran the chariot of Ahab. Unusual things happen when the anointing of God comes upon you.

The anointing gives you access into the secrets of God. It gives you mastery over His mysteries.

Before Adam fell, the anointing was upon him. He could discern the mind of God and was able to name all the animals God had created. In the same way, the anointing upon Jesus caused Him to know all things, and that same anointing is upon you now. Therefore, you, too, can know all things.

The Scriptures show us, in Psalm 89:20-23, that it was that anointing that took David to the throne despite every obstacle. You cannot stop or hinder the anointing of God. It is a force that will bring victory to you every time.

In Luke 4:18-19 is found a key that Jesus used, and things changed. Joel 2:28 says, *"It shall come to pass afterward, that I will pour out my spirit upon all flesh."* God's Spirit is being poured out even now. This is the key to working miracles (see Zechariah 4:6). Let every yoke be broken. Let there be liberty and breakthrough in every life in the name of Jesus Christ.

There are certain things you do in the Kingdom that make so much noise that Heaven cannot rest until your case is resolved. Even when you say nothing, those things speak on your behalf. Situations may not be announced before they come, and they may sometimes take you by surprise, but we have the assurance that there is no way anything can prevail against us as we remain faithful to God (see Acts 10:38-41).

Yes, as I unlock the force of unlimited wonders, my life is enriched, and I can pour out to others. And, yes, you and I must now learn to walk in and live in the fullness of our God-given inheritance.

Shalom!

Righteous Decrees for Life

Father, I receive grace to put You first in everything from today on in the name of Jesus! Help me to seek You with all my heart in Jesus' name!

Father, I take authority now over the days to come and declare that every obstacle in my path be removed! These shall be days, weeks, months, and years of testimony and divine encounter, free of evil in Jesus' name!

Father, I have the key of life and death in my hand! I shut up all the powers of death! Nothing and no one will die prematurely around me henceforth in the name of Jesus! By the blood of Jesus. Death, I lock you up completely and all your forces in Jesus' name!

CHAPTER 10

LIVING A SUCCESSFUL LIFE

A wise man is strong; yea, a man of knowledge increaseth strength.

Proverbs 24:5

Congratulations for being part of the family of God. Your quest for the knowledge of the truth shows me that you are ready to make a change that will affect your destiny forever.

Your connectivity with God will free you from the religious bigotry that holds many in bondage and mediocrity. The purpose of the wings of a bird are so that it can fly, and the fin of the fish is useless if it cannot swim. Your destiny in God is abused if you are not successful and impactful (see Galatians 3:29 and Isaiah 27:6).

But success in life is a function of principles and instructions. Everyone is born to be successful, but not everyone will be successful because not everyone will be committed to the price that has to be paid or the lessons that have to be learned. Here are some important principles to study and put into practice if you desire to live a successful life in Christ.

1. **The principle of inspiration.** Success is all about inspiration. If you are not inspired, you will expire. What drives you determines how far you can go. Life can be boring without an inspiration. When you take your inspiration from the Word of God, you become a living legend. Inspire a man about what he is capable of doing, and you have lighted a fire no one can quench.

    Jesus sought to inspire His disciples about what they were capable of doing (see Mark 11:22-24). He had spoken to a tree, and it responded to His words. "But you," He was telling His disciples, "will speak to mountains, and they will be moved."

When He had gone back to Heaven, they practiced what He had inspired them to do. At the Beautiful Gate, they commanded a man who had been crippled his entire life to get up and walk, and he did (see Acts 3:2-10). Peter heard about a man named Aeneas who was paralyzed and bedridden for eight years. Going to the man's house, Peter spoke healing to him, *"and he arose immediately"* (Acts 9:34). Today, the Word of God is our inspiration (see Mark 9:23 and John 14:12). Paul wrote:

All scripture is given by inspiration of God, and is profitable for doctrine, for reproof, for correction, for instruction in righteousness: that the man of God may be perfect, throughly furnished unto all good works. 2 Timothy 3:16-17

If you never see good in a thing, you are never inspired.

2. **The principle of enthusiasm.** There must be a passion for your destiny. What you

don't have a passion for, you easily give up on. Just a little pressure can take you out. It takes enthusiasm to press on, and you do it because you know what is ahead and have a passion for it.

Enthusiasm is a product of dreams and visions. Enthusiasm is provoked by strong imagination. Everyone has some talent, some gift, but what you do with your talent is based on your enthusiasm. The reason many bury their talents is that they are not very enthusiastic about them (see Matthew 25:14-15 and 18).

Esau lost his position because of a lack of enthusiasm. Abraham was giving glory to God because he was enthusiastic about the promises He had made, and he got them (see Romans 4:20-21 and Psalm 119:162).

Enthusiasm opens you up to having helpers for your destiny. Seeing your convictions makes them want to be part of your vision.

Jesus told a story of a man who found a field that he liked. He was so enthusiastic about it that he sold all that he had and bought the field (see Matthew 13:46). Enthusiasm will silence negative thoughts and negative perceptions and move you forward.

We live in a world of rewards. Be enthusiastic, and someone will reward you. You can be sure that something good is coming your way even now.

3. **The principle of action.** If you believe what God believes about yourself, you will always be on top of things, for you will act on what you believe (see Jeremiah 29:11). Life is not about explanations; it is about a right philosophy that leads to action (see Colossians 2:8). Success in life depends on reasoning like God reasons. It lies in the ability to analyze your ideas and thinking and bring them into line with your dreams, and then act on them.

You cannot blame anyone else for your failures. What you do with what you have is what makes you successful. There is a treasure in you waiting to be explored (see 2 Corinthians 4:7). Your mission is stronger than your obstacles, and God is committed to what He put in your heart, not what stands against you. So put action to your mission, and move toward success.

The only creature that limits its growth and potential is the human. Have you ever seen a tree that refused to grow to its destined height or a cow that refused to grow to full maturity? Only humans limit themselves, and they do it because of what other people say or feel. It's time to go for the prize of the high calling. You are in God's class of being. Take action!

Action is a proof that you believe in who you are and that you know your vision is realizable. What might you do if you knew your dreams could not be stopped? Your desire is a reality. Therefore, you must take steps immediately to see it come to pass.

Develop confidence in your dream today, for *"all things are possible to him* [or her] *that believeth"* (Mark 9:23). When what you face becomes smaller than what you have in your mind, you can crush every obstacle with little or no effort. Take action!

That was how David defeated Goliath. He remembered the lion and the bear, saw Goliath as just another of his conquests and went after him. And what were the results? He won. Action follows when you know that who you are is bigger than what you face. That causes you to take action.

4. **The principle of endurance.** Endurance is not a gift; it's an attitude, a product of insight based on clarity of vision. Gold can be found on Earth, but it is usually not on the surface or easily discovered. It takes some serious digging to get to it, and that digging process requires endurance.

You will probably not find gold with your first shovelful of dirt. Endurance didn't put it there, but endurance can get it out. The Bible says, *"But he that shall endure unto the end, the same shall be saved"* (Matthew 24:13), and the same applies to every other blessing from God.

We are all given by God the promise of greatness, the promise of a decorated destiny, but He cannot give you endurance. Endurance is a product of personal discipline. Those who fall by the wayside also had a place at the top, but they refused to pursue it. If God has not given up on you, why should you give up on yourself? He is the Doer; you are just the representative who cooperates with Him to see the mighty results. Why would you settle for less, when God has destined you for the best? Go for it!

Setbacks should never determine the outcome of your life. They were intended as part of the learning process. Success comes as you obey the Scriptures:

Looking unto Jesus the author and finisher of our faith; who for the joy that was set before him endured the cross, despising the shame, and is set down at the right hand of the throne of God.

Hebrews 12:2

If you lack focus and an expectation, enduring can be frustrating. The good news is that Jesus is always with you in this journey, and He is also waiting for you at the finish line. He knows what it is to endure, and He knows that you, too, with His help, can endure till the end.

5. **The principle of pure motives.** Success is a lot more than having a dream. If you want to accomplish great things with God, check your motives. If your motives are wrong, you will very quickly find that God is not interested in helping you. If what you want to accomplish does not honor God and bless your fellowman, humanity, it is not a dream from God; it is mere fleshly ambition. We were given an unfinished world, and God is trusting us to finish it by using the wisdom He puts in us for each accomplishment. But nothing can be accomplished with wrong motives. Corn won't grow until it is planted, and steel will not extract itself from the iron ore

where it originates. God has given us a part to play in the success of everyday life and provided everything we need to accomplish it. But He will not bless wrong motives.

Jesus told a parable of a rich man who had everything he needed to prosper. However, because of his wrong motives, he suddenly died that same night (see Luke 12:16-20).

God even requires kings to have proper motives:

> *Amaziah was twenty and five years old when he began to reign, and he reigned twenty and nine years in Jerusalem. And his mother's name was Jehoaddan of Jerusalem. And he did that which was right in the sight of the LORD, but not with a perfect heart.*
>
> 2 Chronicles 25:1-2

Jesus gave us a powerful inducement for improvement in this regard (see Matthew 6:33). Every covenant child of God is a living star, born to be successful in all that they do (see Psalm 1:3 and Matthew 5:13-14). It is indeed God's will for every child of His to be successful. He has placed us *above all nations of the earth* (Deuteronomy 28:1-2).

So God's mandate over your life is success, and His mandate of success is holistic. Yours is not to be mere financial success. It is to be spiritual, material, and emotional as well (see 3 John 2). Any failure, therefore, will be a product of choices you make, not the destiny God designed for you (see Deuteronomy 30:19). It is up to each of us, therefore, to live a life of Kingdom success through pure motives.

6. **The principle of self-improvement.** Success is not determined by gifts and talents, but by personal discipline. God gives you grace, but you have to supply the necessary willpower. Many work hard on their job, but they work much less on themselves. When you work hard on your job, you make a living, but when you work hard on yourself, you make a fortune.

No machine produces great results without a good operator. God has given you *"all things that pertain to life and godliness"* (see 2 Peter 1:3-4), but you must be the operator, and that means the first thing you need to work on is yourself. The books you read, the training you get, the appetites you control, and the values you respect all have the potential to earn you the destiny you desire.

When a woman learns to submit to her husband, she is taking a major step toward keeping her man (see Ephesians 5:22). When a man learns to love his wife, he is securing his future with that wife for a stable home and family life (see Ephesians 5:25).

What I have noticed is that people's tastes seem to change with any increase in their financial income. Suddenly, they can't tolerate that smaller TV set and "need" to upgrade their smartphone. Many of the things people buy these days are things they don't even need. Within a few months, they find their place with other cast-off items in storage in the garage, or they are placed in garage sales at much reduced prices. What's happening here? This shows a serious lack of discipline. It shows that we have not taken seriously the need for self-improvement.

Many seem unable to find even thirty minutes a day in their busy schedule to pray, and yet they can't understand it when they come under spiritual attack. You will never escape such attacks. The devil is *"as a roaring lion ... seeking whom he may devour"* (1 Peter 5:8). You need the anointing of God on your life, fresh fire from Heaven, to resist this enemy. If there is no prayer, no fasting, no reading of the Word, and no church attendance, any success you experience will be short-lived. Team up with God, and your success will be eternal. Discipline will bring self-management, and the result will be unlimited success.

7. **The principle of rewards.** Receiving rewards increases your productivity. Have you ever seen the whale display in Sea World in Orlando? With each display,

the whale is rewarded, and so the animal does more and more. Psalm 16:8 declares, *"I have set the LORD always before me, because he is at my right hand I shall not be moved."* If you don't understand that psychologically man responds to rewards, you will stall your progress and performance. For every goal you set for yourself, learn to attach a reward to it, no matter how small, and then follow through.

In school, they give rewards. At work, there are rewards. Even churches give out rewards. If no reward is involved in a matter, you may very well have little or no enthusiasm for it.

If you want to lose weight, for example, set a goal and, with it, include a reward. For example, treat yourself when you have lost a certain number of pounds. If you have a goal for reading good books, attach a reward to that goal. This makes your goals realizable and your journey exciting. Learn to use rewards to your spiritual benefit.

8. **The principle of attraction.** You attract what you become. There is no accidental success. Your thinking becomes your living. If you are a failure, no one else is responsible for it. You attract what you become.

It is very important that we monitor what we hear, see, and say, because what you attract is what you become. Your associations are a big key to your breakthrough in life. *"He that walketh with wise men shall be wise: but the companion of fools shall be destroyed"* (Proverbs 13:20).

If you don't like where you are, just take a look around you at your companions. When men saw Saul prophesying, they said, *"Is Saul also among the prophets?"* (1 Samuel 10:11-12). It is the company you keep that determines your accomplishments.

When you see the grace of God upon someone, don't let pride, arrogance, and competition deny you access to them. Ask them questions, and let the grace and anointing on them rub off on you. If you are too private to relate, you will be privately oppressed. Let yourself be attracted to what you long to become.

9. **The principle of worth.** Increase your value, and you will increase your worth. You are valued for what you bring to the marketplace. You will never be paid $20 an hour if you are not valued at $20 an hour.

God values you, and your fellow believers value you, but maybe the secular marketplace does not. What you bring to the table out in the world determines your value out in the world. The good news is that you can change how people see and value you, for you *"have the mind of Christ"* (1 Corinthians 2:16).

Many people never read another book after they graduate. That alone can decrease your worth by more that ninety-five percent. Continually add to the knowledge you have, and you will remain competitive. Those who are elevated are constantly learning new things.

Many years ago, I was concerned about the state of the Church and decided to seek God about it. To me, the Church of our day did not look like what the Bible described, and I felt that something had to be done. As a result, God put on me a grace to stop the wickedness of Satan and the brutality of his sicknesses and diseases. Through God's anointing, I began adding value to and releasing men and women into their destiny, and the result was that my ministry changed forever. Those I ministered to could no longer remain the same. It was not possible, not because of me, but because of Christ in me who was doing the work. If you will heed what is written here, Satan will be forced to come under your feet permanently in the name of Jesus Christ.

The seasons of life may not change, but you will be able to take advantage of every situation. Strive constantly for more wisdom and Heaven-sent skills. Learn to read and understand the seasons.

Nothing lasts forever. *"Weeping may endure for a night, but joy cometh in the morning"* (Psalm 30:5). Don't frustrate yourself with any one particular season. Know that it is about to change, and success is not what you pursue but what you become by increasing your value, your worth, in the marketplaces of life.

10. **The principle of taking responsibility.** Like many, you may try to dodge responsibility, but you can never dodge the consequences. Many say, "Life is too short." Yes, but their problem is that it has taken them so long to get started. Preparation, position, talents, and practice will sharpen you for the task ahead. It is important that you polish your skills and acquire new ones. The worst enemies of responsibility are procrastination, making excuses, and playing the blame game. Learning the principle of responsibility will set you on the path to success.

As I learn more and more of the biblical secrets of living a successful life, I am fulfilled and become a blessing to others. And, yes, you and I must continue learning to walk in and live in the fullness of our God-given inheritance.

Shalom!

Righteous Decrees for Life

Father, in the name of Jesus Christ, let Your favor open every closed door for me in the days ahead in the name of Jesus!

Father, in the name of Jesus, organize my wonders and send me helpers of destiny in the coming days in Jesus' name!

Father, in the name of Jesus Christ, let Your favor manifest through me to my world in these days in Jesus' name!

AUTHOR CONTACT INFORMATION

You may contact the author directly in the following way:

eMail: Bishopidowu@crepa.org

Telephone: (904) 469-5724